Legacy

A Story in Three Parts

By

Len Manwaring

*To Reeno and Collin
Very best wishes
Len Manwaring*

Rotherfield Studio Ltd

Legacy

A Story in Three Parts

by
Len Manwaring

Copyright information

All rights reserved. No part of this publication may be reproduced, stored in a retrieval system, rebound or transmitted in any form or for any purpose without the prior written permission of the author and publisher. This book is sold subject to the condition that it shall not be lent, resold, hired out or otherwise circulated without the publisher's prior consent in any form or binding other than that which it is published.

ISBN 978-0-9566304-1-4

First Published July 2011
Rotherfield Studio Ltd

Text Set in Bembo by Rotherfield Studio Ltd
E-mail sales@rotherfieldstudio.com

Registered Office 14 Wellington Square Hastings East Sussex, TN34 1PB

Printed in England by Berforts Group Ltd, Hastings

Acknowledgements

Many people and friends have helped in the preparation of this book and I am grateful for their help and advice. I also wish to acknowledge the help I found in

Williamson, Gordon. German E boats, 1939-1945. Osprey, 2002.

Ordnance Survey. Canterbury and the Isle of Thanet, Sheet 150. 2007.

I am especially grateful to Ian Streeter who read the manuscript with meticulous care and pointed out many errors. I am appreciative of his knowledge of the date regarding the invention of the laptop. As a result Kit has now been given a portable typewriter. Motor bikes did not have twin headlamps at the time of my story and Pauline would have worn ordinary clothes, not leathers. However, with a bit of poetic licence and Ian's grudging approval, I have decided to keep to the original script.

I am pleased to record my thanks to my publisher, Frank Ball, of Rotherfield Studio Ltd for his help and guidance.

Elizabeth, my wife, drew the maps and did the illustrations. Thank you Elizabeth, they enhance the book.

Dedication

This is for Andy, my favourite son-in-law, who is also my friend.

Thanks for all your help, Son!

Contents

Part 1
Thanet Assignment

Prologue 3

Map of North-East Kent 4
1   A Bed for the Night 5
2   Girl Biker 15
3   Down to Work 25
4   Accidental Meeting 33
5   Cards on the Table 43
6   Two Down 51
7   Weekend Break 59
8   Return to London 65
9   Learning about Boats and Justice 71

Part 2
Escape to Freedom

Prologue 77

Map of North Holland 78
German E boat at speed 78
10 A Chance Re-Union 79
11 A Bold Plan 83
12 A Bagful of Trouble 87
13 Boating with the Enemy 91
14 No Turning Back 97
15 The Royal Navy Arrives 101
16 Helping Hands 105
Receipt for the E boat 108
17 Safe at last 111
18 Married 117

Part 3
The Curious Affair at Plucks Gutter

Prologue		123
Map of The Isle of Thanet		124
19	Thanet is an Island	125
20	Rendezvous on the River	129
21	River of Mud	133
22	Raised Voices	137
23	Salvage Operations	141
24	Proof of Ownership	147
25	The Captain's Testimony	151
26	The River Relents	157
27	Wedding Bells	163
Author's Note		169

Part 1
Thanet Assignment

Prologue

Christopher Tynan is a freelance journalist, hoping some day to have time to write a novel that has been buzzing around in his head for years. He's neither rich nor poor and for the moment is content to pursue his present vocation. This involves travelling round the country and writing about local customs, characters and places. Occasionally these become expanded into historical stories and social events of the region under review. As a result of fairly extensive travel within the British Isles he has acquired a useful knowledge of topical tales. This led, a few years ago, to the publication of a series of slim volumes entitled 'Friendly Invaders' which was well received and another on 'Local legends and Customs' which has yet to receive recognition.

In recent years he has contributed to a few local brochures, highlighting local interests in order to persuade visitors to follow up the stories by spending some time in the area. Christopher often works under contract for Max Sutherland, the features editor of Capital News. This newspaper publishes special issues twice a year with Christopher as one of its main contributors on local interest stories. As far as Tynan is concerned each assignment follows closely a pattern established over the years, until now. On this occasion his visit to Margate has a double purpose...

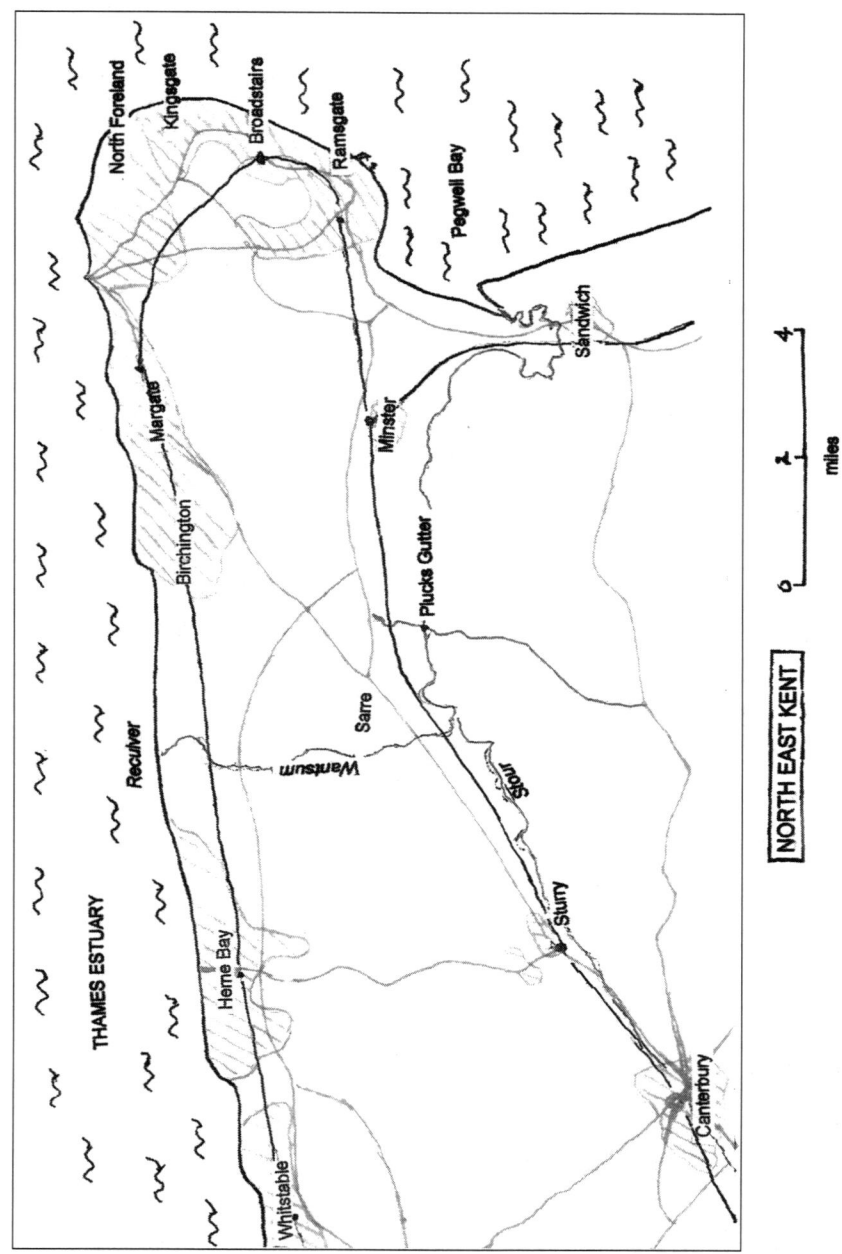

Chapter 1   A Bed for the Night

As soon as he moved from the platform into the lofty waiting room he knew it had been a mistake to travel down to Margate by train. A seaside town towards the end of the season is not the best of places to be without personal transport. Yet looking back on events that had landed him in his present predicament Christopher was almost convinced that fate has much more to answer for than most people realise. More to the point it was his editor who had almost insisted that he travel down without delay. This meant leaving his car that had only just gone in for a major service. Then again it hadn't been his editor whose job was concerned with general features. No, it had been the crime editor who had persuaded him just this once to carry out an additional assignment as a favour.

On the face of it he could scarcely refuse. He had a contract with the features editor to provide three articles a year ranging from social history to local follies and from ancient and more recent invaders to visits by royalty in the eighteenth and nineteenth centuries. The present article was to be included in the January issue of the supplement and was to highlight local pleasure gardens of bygone Margate and Ramsgate and to feature their modern counterparts. It was also to be linked to the publication of the local brochure issued by the local publicity department. Tynan had done similar articles for many east coast resorts.

In the past he had tried out several different approaches in order to get the feel of the place before putting pen to paper. Sometimes he already knew a little about the place but occasionally his visits required extensive research. This time he knew only the bare bones of the area. It was his first venture into the Thanet towns and he had been looking forward to covering new ground.

He was known by some of his journalist friends as Kit and often signed pieces with the initials KT. Many years ago he had come across a particularly good recipe for ham and sausage pie that he had enjoyed at a farmhouse and purely as an addition to an article had included it suitably modified with an ingredient of his own. This was presented as the work of Katie and it had proved popular. KT, as a pseudonym, had then been suggested by his editor and Christopher couldn't really see any objection. From then on, once a year, he had added a new recipe from a different part of the country and two years ago these had been gathered together into 'KATIE KOOKS, a slim volume which helped to keep the wolf from the door. Some assumed Katie was his wife. Others thought it was his sister. Neither assumption was correct for he was an only child and not married although. He did like to cook when time permitted.

A few days before he was due to start this latest assignment, Max, the features editor, had asked him to call round and on entering his office had been introduced to Howard Marshall, the Crime Buster as he was known. Marshall came straight to the point. 'You've heard about this spate of sabotage that's been going on all along the east coast?'

'Yes,' replied Kit. 'I thought it must be someone with a grudge. Now I'm not sure. There have been too many incidents for it to be the work of one individual.'

'You're right there,' replied Howard. 'All my reporters are covering the east coast resorts. Max tells me you are off to Margate gathering material for one of your articles.'

'Yes. That's right. I'm off next week, Monday in fact, as soon as I can collect my car. It's just been in for a major service. Why?'

'There was an incident at Margate yesterday and Ramsgate would be the next obvious target if our friend runs to form. Could you delay your own research for a couple of days and help to cover this new outbreak? We'll make it worth your while.'

'Well I really don't know. I've no experience of this sort of thing,' replied Kit, already becoming interested with the idea.

'It's no big deal,' explained Marshall. 'As soon as Sutton and King are free they'll come down and take over. I need someone from this paper to put in an appearance as soon as possible.'

Kit knew he was weakening but felt he should not give in too easily so played hard to get a little longer. 'What,' he wanted to know, 'would I be expected to provide in the way of copy and would it be my by-line?'

'No problem,' replied Howard. 'If you come across anything of interest let us know. You'll have a new slant on it anyway. Send your copy as usual and we'll tighten it up if necessary. Give it a whirl and thanks.'

'O.K. If you're sure I can handle it.'

'Fine. There's just one more thing. Can you go today? As your car is in dock can you go by train? Make an inconspicuous arrival.' He handed Kit a small document saying, 'Keep this with your press card and show it to the police if necessary.' With a quick wave he was gone.

Thinking back Kit was surprised how easily he had been persuaded. Now, though he was quite looking forward to this new challenge, he had been tempted to wait and go by his car on Monday but Max had finally persuaded him to keep to the agreement. So here he was in this empty waiting room several hours later than had been suggested by the time-table. The train was very late, even for this region, having been delayed twice. Once was just outside Chatham for half an hour. The second time was for three hours due to power lines having fallen across the track a few miles down towards the coast.

Going by train Kit appreciated that he saw more of the countryside except that in this part of the country everything look a bit flat. The last of the North Downs had disappeared under the tunnel at Chatham and now well past Sittingbourne the Kentish countryside seemed boring. Even the wooded parts presented little in the way of interest. Another month and the autumn tints might have made a difference but at last the train drew into Margate station. Kit gathered up his bag, his portable typewriter and made for the exit. Three other passengers got off and disappeared into the gathering dusk.

Passing quickly out of the station the north wind nearly blew him back inside as he opened the door leading directly onto the seafront. There were no taxis so he returned to the relative calm of the waiting hall and enquired from the ticket office about other means of transport into town.

'You've picked a bad day,' was the comment. 'Wednesday is early closing and there are few taxis on call today. Those that were available have come out in sympathy with the buses that are on strike. They might be back tomorrow.'

Kit made his way to the buffet. At the moment it seemed to be the only bright spot in town although he didn't much fancy British Rail tea. The waitress smiled as he entered and then the smile changed perceptibly. As he got closer to the counter she gave him a long searching look as though she recognised him but could not quite remember. 'Tea please,' he said in answer to her, 'What can I get you?'

The tea was fresh and hot and he realised it had just been made in a tea-pot. 'Is there anything to eat?' he enquired. 'Yes. We do an all day breakfast. Lunch is usually a meat pie or roast. There's fish or salad and cold meat.' He opted for bacon, sausage and egg, suddenly realising it was several hours since he had last eaten and that too had been breakfast.

'Go over to the window and I'll bring it along when its ready.'

'Thanks,' replied Kit and moved over to a table, the only one laid and which also sported a table lamp.

His meal arrived within ten minutes. 'I've put some bread and butter as well and here's another cup of tea. O.K.?'

'Thanks very much.' The waitress busied herself setting it down before him with practised ease though all the while looking at him intently. As soon as he caught her glance she looked away. The meal was enjoyable. Kit thought to himself, 'You can't really go wrong with bacon and egg,' and he had been very hungry. As soon as he'd finished he walked over to the telephone box to look for a hotel to spend the night. Normally he would have done this in advance but the circumstances of this trip had made him forget. The first three hotels had no vacancies. Two others answered but said they had closed for the season while three others never bothered to answer.

A new waitress arrived, smiled at him as he sat down again at the table and contemplated his next move. She also stared at him as though she knew him. He caught her glance and held it while she said, 'Sorry. I thought I knew you.'

Her features were similar to the waitress who had cooked his meal, a mother perhaps or a much older sister. 'May I leave my things here? I need to go along to the shops.'

'Yes. That's all right I'll look after them for you.'

'Thanks.'

It was good to get outside even though it was still blowing a gale. He'd heard about these winds that hit the north Kent coast and seemed to come directly from the Arctic. He appreciated that the tall buildings on both sides of the road created a venturi effect and forced the wind along at an even greater pace. Even so he thought a walk along the sea front would clear away the cobwebs so he moved down towards the beach in front of the Nayland Rock Hotel. However, after no more than five minutes he was glad when just before he reached the old Sea Bathing Hospital, he turned away from the sea and found a few shops in a road running parallel to the coast. Only two remained open, a tobacconist-cum-sweet shop and a florist. Although he rarely smoked he had got into the habit of usually carrying a packet of cigarettes especially on research outings. Offering a cigarette still broke down barriers. Having bought cigarettes and matches and an evening paper he spoke again to the man behind the counter.

'I've left it a bit late to find a room for the night. Do you happen to know where I might get a bed for the night?'

'Not around here. They've all gone off to Spain for their winter holidays. Some of the hotels are still open but they will be full. There's a big conference here in the closed season. You might be lucky with a B and B but I don't know of any offhand. Hope the weather improves for you.'

'Thanks. I'll take some of those boiled sweets and this book.' Having selected a crime novel he went out into the blustery night and came to a bus shelter out of the wind. Glancing through the adverts he saw very few vacancies and most were for long term renting. His refuge was not as sheltered as he had thought so after a few minutes he walked across the road to a garage. Maybe he could hire a car.

'Sorry,' was the greeting he received. 'The office is closed for the day. We're only open for petrol.' 'Call tomorrow,' was the parting shot of the attendant. There was nothing for it but to return to the station, collect his things and walk into town looking for somewhere to stay. The older woman had gone leaving the younger and prettier one in charge. She recognised him but again there was that questioning look as though she knew him. He searched back through his memory but felt sure he had never seen her before.

There was no one else in the restaurant and by way of breaking the ice he asked her about the lack of taxis. She explained that it was the end of the season, and there was to be a take over of the local bus company when many drivers would be laid off. For two days the present drivers had been on strike and had received support from the local population. Even the taxi drivers had joined in although one might have supposed they would relish the extra business a bus strike would bring them.

Again she gave him that long questioning look, almost waiting for him to make some comment. To fill what might have been an awkward silence he asked if she knew of any vacancies for the night, explaining how so far he had been unsuccessful. 'I'm not sure,' came her reply and then disappeared. On her return, a few minutes later, she continued with the conversation as though she had never left. 'Most of the big hotels are full. There's a large engineering conference here. With luck the strike will be over in a day or so and the reporters will have also gone.'

Should he tell her that he, too, was a reporter looking for a story, not about engineers or strikes but something possibly more sinister. Instead he said, 'I've just walked along to the garage and tried to hire a car without success.'

He hoped his reply would be sufficient for the time being. As he spoke he tried to guess her age. It could be twenty, probably not as old as thirty, more like twenty- five. If the older woman was the mother then twenty-five was most likely correct. A very pretty woman with long black wavy hair and a ready smile playing round her lips. She wore hardly any makeup, expertly applied so that it accentuated her features. He really couldn't decide the colour of her eyes in this light, possibly dark blue or hazel. Bubbling with life would be an accurate description, he thought, although that would convey nothing of her physical appearance.

She busied herself behind the counter, collecting cups and saucers and then glanced once more in his direction. 'What are you doing down here at this time of the year?' He'd never thought about lying but the abruptness of the question threw him off guard. In the space of a split second he considered a half-truth would suffice. 'I'm a free lance journalist down here to prepare a feature for the town's brochure for next year.' At least that part was true.

'Oh. That's interesting,' came the response yet he felt she did not quite believe him so he continued, 'The main article will be featured in a supplement to Capital News early next year. I usually book a room well in advance but this time I got delayed and took a chance. Wish I'd stayed at home now. However as I'm here I'll press on.'

She didn't pursue her line of questioning but asked, 'How long are you going to stay here?'

'Oh. I'll go in a minute.'

'I mean how long are you likely to stay in Margate?'

'Oh. It will be just a few days. Maybe to the end of the week but I've got to find a bed for the night. I don't really want to return to London so I'd better make a move towards town now.'

'If you don't mind staying out of town you can come back with me for a few days.'

The unspoken question on his face made her burst into laughter.

'No. Not that. My parents have plenty of room. They run a small holiday adventure centre called The Haven. It's mainly during the spring and summer but there's usually a small section open all year round. It's up to you.'

'That really is most kind of you. Is that who you phoned just now?'

'Yes. I wanted to make sure they could take you.'

'Thanks for the offer. I'll gladly accept but how do I get there?'

'You can come back with me when I leave here at 6.30. My aunt, the lady you first saw when you arrived will be back then until ten o'clock when we close.'

He tried once more to express his thanks but she dismissed them saying, 'It's not free but it's not expensive. They will look after you alright.'

By now the time had crept almost to six o'clock. 'Should I have another meal here before we go or will there be an evening meal at The Haven?'

'Depends how hungry you are. I'd be inclined to leave it until we get home.'

'That's what I'll do then. I'll just go along to the shops and get a few things. I'll be back in twenty minutes.'

'O.K. I'll see you.' She began cooking eggs and bacon for a group of railway staff that had suddenly appeared. Obviously it was a standing order.

Christopher suddenly felt the frustration of the past few hours ebbing away. He was no longer bothered at not having previously found somewhere to stay or even that the local transport seemed to be in short supply. He was still annoyed, mainly with himself for not having his own car as he always did on these assignments. He had agreed to travel by train solely on the wishes of the crime editor although he later discovered the order had come from the editor in chief and later still he was to find out exactly why.

The wind was still blowing and lifting particles of sand as he made his way back to the newsagents where he purchased a small box of candies. Then it was on to the florists where he bought a small bunch of freesias and begged a small cardboard box to prevent them getting too crushed. He also got the phone number of the garage so he'd be able to hire a car the next day.

He used a public telephone to call Max, explaining what had happened so far and that his report would not be sent until the following evening at the earliest. 'No problem,' came the immediate and totally unexpected response. 'Enjoy yourself. The other reporters from the opposition haven't got anything either. You're already two days late. Not your fault I know so another day is not going to make much difference.' But there was an edge to his voice that did not fit in with his normal easy-going ways.

'May I remind you,' began Kit, 'I'm not a reporter. I'm only doing this as a favour to you. If you don't like it let's forget the whole thing.' He couldn't understand why he was taking out his returning frustration on poor old Max.

'Now, now. Don't take on so. Just testing. See you soon.' With that the click on the phone told him the conversation had been terminated. Kit was convinced his editor was not alone in the office. Over the years he reckoned that the editors portrayed in films was fairly accurate. They were all, with the possible exception of Max Sutherland, hard bitten businessmen.

Few had any real scruples, only wanting to reach deadlines if possible before rival firms and with little feeling for people involved with the stories. Max was the one exception, who by the very nature of his department, possibly had a more leisurely role to fulfil. This reflected in his attitude to life and to dealings with his staff – that is until now. It seemed that even he was beginning to be tarred with the same editorial brush, or was it brushed with editorial tar. Kit smiled at his own joke.

Once more relaxed and feeling strangely pleased with himself Kit Tynan walked slowly back to the station, collected his overnight bag and put his recent purchases inside also picked up his typewriter and waited for his lift to the night's lodging. It was 6.25 and the girl's aunt arrived to do her evening stint. He was acutely aware that he didn't know her name or that of the girl.

'Pauline,' called out the aunt, 'I'm here so you can get off home.' So the niece was Pauline. Amazing what you can find out by just listening. Perhaps by the end of this assignment he would find out more than if he posed searching questions. He had no real idea how to proceed and considered phoning Max to tell him to forget the whole thing. Pauline appeared briefly, said goodbye to her aunt and then spoke to Kit. 'I'll see you at the front of the station in a few minutes. O.K.?'

'Yes. Thanks.' Picking up his luggage Kit said goodnight to the aunt and went out into darkening night.

Chapter 2   Girl Biker

While waiting for his chauffeuse to arrive Kit considered what type of car this laughing girl might drive. Would it be a smart refurbished MG sports, a battered Morris Traveller or an old Land Rover. On balance he thought the MG would suit her best. Then out of the gloom a roar greeted his ears and twin headlamps cut the darkness as Pauline arrived astride a 500cc motor-bike with bits of her hair sticking out from beneath her helmet. The roar diminished to a quiet murmur as she slowed down and stopped beside him. She stood the bike up, went inside the station and came out with her aunt's helmet for Kit.

She made no comment regarding her mode of transport but equal to the occasion and beginning to enjoy the unusual situation Kit said nothing but merely took the proffered spare helmet. It took a few seconds to adjust his headgear and sit astride the bike as a pillion passenger. But his heart was pounding as he contemplated a nightmare journey into the country.

'I'll take your bag and strap it on the front and you can put your briefcase in the left hand pannier.' Pauline took his bag and fastened it over the petrol tank.

'O.K,' she called. 'Hold on. We're off.'

Hold on he did, tentatively at first but with growing confidence in her handling of the big machine he realised it might not be such a bad trip after all. It was years since he'd ridden a motor-bike and even longer since he'd been on the back as a pillion passenger. At a steady speed they went down the station approach towards the sea and then a sharp right and under the railway bridge, left at the T junction and then along Hartsdown Road with the football ground way over on the right. A quick change down the gears to ease the engine as it climbed to the top of the hill coming to a gentle stop to let other traffic pass. The momentum of even such a gentle stop pushed him forwards towards the rider. As soon as the road was clear she accelerated and he clung closer, feeling her supple body beneath her clothes.

She gave no conscious acceptance of his closer hold and as the built-up area gave way to more open countryside the speed increased. The nearness of the hedges on the left as they sped past and being so close to the ground accentuated the speed although he felt no fear, merely exhilaration. In no time at all, it seemed, the speed decreased as she moved into a lower gear. With a toot on the horn

Pauline guided the bike through an open gate and on to the forecourt in front of a house. As he relaxed and withdrew his arms from around her waist and dismounted she said cheekily, 'There you are sir. All safely delivered. I'll bring your case inside later.' He dismounted, stood silently by the front door, removed his helmet and handed it to her smiling his thanks and retrieved his typewriter from the pannier.

Christopher watched as the girl disappeared on her bike round the side of the house while he stood inside the porch then rang the bell and went inside. A woman came towards him and for a moment he thought it was the same one who had served him at the station. However, a second later he realised this woman, although obviously related, was appreciably less well endowed and with features much more relaxed and friendly.

'Hello,' she greeted him. 'I'm Pauline's mother. You must be the orphan from the station.'

'Yes. I'm Christopher Tynan and I'm most grateful to you for putting me up for the night.'

'No problem. Not many people here this time of the year. Come on through and sign the register.' Once these formalities had been completed she added, 'You can either stay here in the main house or you can have one of the chalets.'

'Here will be fine.'

'A wise choice on a night like this. The chalets have all got central heating but here in the house we have a nice log fire as well. Here we are then. Room 3. It's through the hall and up a small flight of stairs then the first door on the left. It's self-contained and here's the key.'

'Thanks.'

'When you're ready come through to the restaurant and we'll see about an evening meal.'

He had just closed the door behind him when there was a knock and Pauline appeared with his case. He wanted her to stay and chat but she disappeared as quickly as she had arrived. A quick shower got rid of the grime of the day and he made his way downstairs having first retrieved the flowers and candies from his bag. As he reached the hall a man came out from the lounge and said, 'Good evening. Travelled far?'

'No, only down from London. By the way what's the lady's name?'

'Same as mine. Matthews. She's my wife, Beryl and I'm Bert.'

'I'm glad to know you. I'm Christopher Tynan.'

'We're fairly informal here especially out of season. Come inside and have a drink. What would you like?'

'I'll have a scotch and water please.' They sat down near the log fire sipping their drinks and chatting about nothing in particular until Matthews suddenly asked Kit what he did for a living and what on earth he was doing down here at this time of the year. Kit felt a little awkward and under normal circumstances would have told him. Now he had to remember exactly what he had told Pauline when she had posed the same question. He took another sip from his drink and coughed as though it had gone down the wrong way. The ruse worked for Bert was all concern for his guest. Kit finished his drink and said, 'My round now. Can I get you the same?'

'No. One's my lot and yours was on the house but I can get you another if you like.'

'No I'm all right. Thanks.'

'Ah. Here's Beryl. She'll want to know what you'd like for dinner.'

'Hello Bert. I didn't hear you come in.'

'Well you wouldn't. I've got my creepers on,' pointing to his rubber-soled shoes.

'Mr Tynan. What would you like to eat? You can have Dover sole or lamb chop.'

'Why don't you offer him some of your steak and kidney pudding,' suggested Bert.

'Well, yes if you'd prefer that you're welcome to try it.'

'That sounds delightful. Thank you.'

'It's almost ready if you'd like to sit at the table in the corner of the restaurant.'

Kit moved away from the warmth of the fire towards the other room when he remembered the flowers. 'I hope you don't mind. These are for you,' offering the spray of freesias.

'Now watch it my lad. Beryl, he's after second helpings already,' suggested Bert.

Kit continued, 'Would you give these to Pauline, please. Just a little thank you for finding me a bed and actually getting me here.'

Beryl, not used to accepting flowers from strangers was momentarily at a loss but quickly recovered to murmur her thanks before disappearing into the kitchen.

'Good move, that,' said Bert. 'I'll see you later.' With that he too left the lounge.

Christopher Tynan suddenly felt awkward. It had only been chit-chat but it was obviously friendly and sincere. In fact since arriving at Margate he had experienced mixed fortunes yet from this family nothing but kindness and help. He felt guilty about not telling Bert his reason for being here and resolved to tell him at least one of the reasons for his visit to Margate out of season. The evening meal was a simple affair. The main course was obviously home made and accompanied by vegetables, beautifully cooked and exactly the meal for a night like this. Kit was glad when the sweet was a choice of fruit salad, ice cream or cheese and biscuits.

Kit felt a bit self-conscious being the only occupant of the restaurant and was surprised when he noticed it was almost 7.30. Pauline came in to thank him for the candies. She had obviously changed and although easily recognisable had altered her appearance in a number of subtle ways. It was still difficult to judge her age - at least 20 but more likely to be 25 with the assurance of a woman of the world. He thought back to when he had been that age and was convinced he had not been so self-assured.

Returning to the warmth of the fire in the lounge he glanced through the paper he had bought, this time reading the news. The sabotage stories were on the front page and it was obvious that local reporters had got on to it in a big way. It seemed that two men had arrived by train yesterday, had coffee in the station buffet and had then hired the only taxi available. They had been followed by another man who had complained about the lack of taxis and then walked off into town. He had told the station staff that the first two were fugitives and that he was anxious to apprehend them. After he had gone someone phoned the police and they had asked for descriptions of all three men. No good details were printed in the paper. A vague description of the two men was given and a slightly better of the third man although all were so vague that they could be applied to hundreds of passengers. Now it seemed that all three were missing.

However the local police were hot on the trail of the first two who had travelled by taxi to Pegwell Bay to catch the Hover ferry to France, or so the taxi driver had told them when questioned. This was obviously not true for all the ferries had been searched without success. The two men appeared to have gone to ground. One thing had occurred, common to other events that had been happening along the east coast. Two sheds had been set alight, not causing any real damage although the emergency services had been drawn away on the hoax. At the end of the report in the paper Kit saw the names of Audrey Sinclair as the manageress of the buffet and her temporary assistant, Pauline Matthews, who had witnessed the arrival of all three men.

Kit went to his room and put in a quick call to his editor and without divulging too much indicated that he had made some progress. Well it was partially true and he hoped to get more information from Pauline if the opportunity presented itself. Having unpacked and spent a few minutes adding notes to his typewriter he reckoned he'd done enough for the day. Since acquiring this new toy a few months ago he had found it extremely useful. Gone were the half remembered notes and trying to decipher his shorthand. Although he now needed to crystallize his thoughts before typing. Occasionally he still used a small pocket tape recorder and thanked his lucky stars that he lived in the electronic age.

Kit returned to the lounge where he had left his paper and found Bert glancing through it. 'Rum do, this,' was his opening remark

'I bought that earlier today. Didn't know your daughter was involved at the time of course. I've only just made the connection,' replied Kit. Then to get away from the subject he enquired, 'Bert, is there a garage nearby where I might hire a car in the morning?'

'Yes. If you go to the end of the lane and turn left, you'll be in the main road. There's a choice of two. If you like we could go there now. One of them stays open quite late so you may be lucky. I usually take the dog for a walk about this time.'

They set off, with Bessie leading the way while they chatted about the weather, the political situation and the report in the paper. It was obviously very much on Bert's mind as he mentioned it twice during their short walk to the garage. It was still open but they had no cars available until the weekend. The second garage was shut so they returned by a different route and stopped at a pub on the main road. Bessie, the dog, had obviously been there before and made straight for the public bar, contemplating a few sips of beer and no doubt some crisps which she invariably got from the customers.

'Evening Bert. Come for your beer?' was the welcome from the man at the bar, followed by half a dozen from others in the room. 'Hello Bess. Want some beer?' The men greeted the dog as she walked towards the assembled company. Out came a heavy glass ashtray into which was poured beer from several of the drinkers. No more encouragement was needed for Bess who walked slowly towards the treat wagging her tail.

'What'll you have young man?'

'I'll try a cider and Bert will have his usual,' replied Kit.

The smiles on the drinkers ceased abruptly as, turning from the antics of the dog, they saw for the first time the man who had come in with Bert. It was only a moment and then the conversation continued although Kit realised he was the subject of their discussion. He turned to Bert. 'What's the problem Bert?'

'I'm afraid you are,' replied Bert. He picked up the late evening paper that had been delivered and hid it quickly under his coat. 'Drink up Kit and we'll talk about it when we get back.'

A few minutes later, with a cheery farewell from Bert they were outside and on their way back home. The three walked slowly along the main road and then down the lane, Bess no doubt wondering why her walk had been cut short. Once inside Bert said, 'Come into the lounge,' and then continued, 'Don't take this the wrong way but do you have any documents to prove who you say you are?'

'Yes. Of course. I've got my driving licence and press card. You can phone my boss if you wish. Why?'

'You know the bloke who disappeared with the other two who arrived at Margate yesterday. Well, have you seen him?'

'Two answers. No. I don't know him and I've never seen him. Why do you ask?'

'Come and look in the mirror,' and with that he practically dragged Kit over to the mirror above the fireplace. Looking at his reflection Kit said, 'That's me.'

'Then who is this?' asked Bert, holding up the paper he had purloined from the pub. On the front page was a police artist's impression of the stranger, now reported missing and who looked so much like Kit it was difficult to laugh it off. Only one thing differed between the two of them. Kit did not have a moustache. He could almost hear Bert's mind ticking over as he appreciated that if the man in the picture had shaved off his moustache it would be an even better likeness of Kit.

'Oh, I see the problem,' was all Kit could utter in reply. 'Look Bert. Here's my identification and I would feel happier if you would phone my boss now so that we can clear this up.'

Bert took the proffered document but refused to telephone Capital News. Instead he handed the card back saying, 'This will do but you must admit it did look suspicious.'

'Well yes but they say everyone has a double somewhere. Tomorrow I need to see the publicity people in Margate. I'm down here to do a piece for next year's brochure. Come with me. The publicity manager will vouch for me even though I am a few days earlier than intended.' Kit went on to explain how he'd done similar articles for other resorts. This time he was hoping to include stories about smugglers and notorious people of the past. Excusing himself for a few minutes Kit went back to his room and returned with a copy of *Katie Kooks* that he usually carried with him. Bert Matthews was finally convinced saying, 'My wife's got a copy of that. She bought it last year.'

'It's a small world,' replied Kit. 'I think I'll make it an early night if you don't mind. There's a lot to get done tomorrow and this picture might complicate things.'

'Goodnight. Breakfast is from 8.00 onwards. Just come down when you're ready. I'll explain things to Beryl.'

'Goodnight and thanks.'

In his room Kit turned over in his mind the events of the day. On the face of it there was nothing really to set it apart from any other day. Delays on rail journeys happen all the time. Mistaken identities also occur from time to time and yet there was something that set alarm bells ringing in his mind. Could it be that somehow Marshall Howard had been aware of the similarity between Kit and one of the men who had since vanished. How could he possibly know before the publication of the photo-fit picture had been printed? What was it all about and why had Howard deliberately exposed him without a hint of what he might encounter? Was he, himself over-reacting regarding these unanswered questions? He lay on the bed turning over and over in his mind the points as they arose. His reverie was interrupted by a knock at his door and Bert's measured tones coming through the panelling. 'Mr. Tynan. Can I come in for a minute?'

'Yes. Just a minute,' and Kit scrambled off the bed and opened the door. 'Come in.'

'Sorry to disturb you,' said Bert. 'Obviously I've mentioned this business to Beryl and we both accept your explanation but you must admit it's all a bit strange. Would you mind if I came with you tomorrow when you go to see that chap?'

'Not at all. You can come in your own right or pretend to be my photographer. I'll give Mr Eastwood a ring first thing and tell him to expect two of us.'

Bert seemed pleased with this arrangement and was about to leave when Kit asked if he would mind if he asked Pauline if she could add anything to what had been reported in the paper. 'You never know something may occur to her and I could join in the hunt for the missing man or men.'

'She's on early shift at the station tomorrow but she'll be here in the afternoon.'

Kit felt he should make some comment about the motorbike. 'I was most impressed by her bike and the way she handled it. Has she been riding long?'

'Nearly three years now. In term time she travels to Canterbury. She's at the university there. At the moment until term starts she's earning a little extra pocket money.'

There were lots of questions Kit would like to have posed but for the moment he let them pass, said goodnight to Bert and closed the door. Tomorrow looked like being an interesting day. He would have to go through the motions of getting details for his forthcoming articles and how the publicity manager required the brochure to be handled. Already this part of his assignment was beginning to take second place. He resolved to tell Bert that because of his own likeness to one of the men that he would follow up the story. This would then explain any interest he might show in the case. The events of the day gradually faded from his troubled mind and he drifted off into a dreamless sleep.

Chapter 3 Down to Work

The grey dawn gave way to a bright day. The north wind had moved round to the east so that although it was cool for mid September it was an improvement on the previous day. Kit entered the restaurant about half past eight and went directly to the single table set for one. A daily paper neatly folded by the table napkin invited early inspection so Kit duly obliged. The stories about the sabotage acts were reported at great length. The earlier ones that had occurred along the east coast were mentioned and comparisons made between them and the latest fires in the Thanet area. The mystery man or someone like him had figured in most operations or had been seen immediately afterwards. There had also been one or two others, variously described as accomplices, rogues and occasionally as plain clothes policemen who were attempting to apprehend the villain.

The descriptions did not always tally and Kit wondered if there could be more than one mystery man. So far there appeared to have been no loss of life resulting from the innumerable acts of sabotage. Some of the buildings had been derelict on private land while most were on government land. Much was made of the time taken up by the emergency services in dealing with these outbreaks when they might be needed elsewhere. At the end of the report a brief notice called attention to the photo-fit picture issued in yesterday's evening paper and stated that it was inaccurate and misleading.

While Kit was considering the significance of this denial Beryl appeared and asked if he'd slept alright and enquired what he'd like for breakfast.

'Good morning, Mrs. Matthews. Toast, tea, egg and bacon will do very nicely, thank you. Is Bert around?'

'Yes. He's been up since six and gone out but he'll be back by 9.0 o'clock. He's driving you into Margate later.'

Kit wondered about broaching the subject uppermost in his mind but decided to tackle Bert first without involving the rest of the family. When he did appear Kit said 'Good morning. I see you had a word with my editor after all about my picture in the paper.'

For a couple of seconds Bert didn't catch on to the allusion but with a smile then replied, 'Yes I told him and also the police that it couldn't possibly be you and in any case I was keeping an eye on you.'

'Thanks a lot. You're not are you? Keeping an eye on me!'

'No of course not and I didn't phone anyone. What do you think it means?' Bert wanted to know.

'Your guess is as good as mine. No doubt all will be revealed eventually. For the moment I've got a job of work to do. Do you still want to come with me?'
'It'll make a change. So yes. I'll tag along if its still alright with you.'

'Just one thing, Bert. Well two really. Please call me Kit or Christopher and you must let me pay for the petrol.'

'O.K. Kit. There's no charge for the petrol. It's a Land Rover and its diesel,' replied Bert with a grin. He seemed to enjoy his little joke and Kit didn't object so just after 9.0 he rang the publicity manager to arrange a meeting that morning if possible. Having agreed, Mr. Eastward said if Kit and his photographer would come at 10. 0 o'clock he had a free slot until noon. On the way to the Council offices Bert gave a running commentary on the route he was taking. 'Well go to the main road, past the pub where we were last night and then along the main road to Margate. The offices are just off Cecil Square and I know he has another office at the Winter Gardens on the sea front in Cliftonville.'

The traffic was fairly light and in just a few minutes Bert found a parking place close to the offices. It took them another five minutes to find the actual room but they were in good time. A young man approached and said, 'Mr. Tynan. Mr. Eastward is ready for you now if you'll come this way.'

Kit had learned from past experience to judge a man's position in any hierarchy by the size of his office. If his theory held true now Mr. Eastward was extremely important for they were shown into a large room, sumptuously furnished and having probably the only decent outlook in the whole building. It looked out onto a neatly tended public garden. The formalities over, Mr. Eastward came straight to the purpose in hand. It seemed that while his staff felt they were quite competent to write the material for themselves there had been a change in policy recently and with the new organization taking place they were overwhelmed with work.

They needed someone to put into words items of local information to highlight aspects of the town and its facilities in order to attract more visitors. The factual evidence needed to be shown in a positive and descriptive narrative that would bring in guests to stay for a week or so as well as day-trippers.

'That's no problem for me,' Kit replied and went on. 'There are two ways of doing this. You can give me a draft and I'll flesh it out or you can tell me roughly what you'd like and I'll collect my own facts and prepare copy for you. You can amend it as you wish but I'd like to see the final draft. I'm also doing a piece for Capital News to go into one of their special issues and that will go out under my own name. The two articles will cover the same ground but I can write them as though they have been written by two different people.'

Mr. Eastward considered this for a moment before replying. 'I don't think it matters if the two articles are similar. I will give you a rough idea of the points I wish you to cover and those of special interest.'

'O.K.,' said Kit. 'You are the client and you choose what you want. I write about places as I see them so inevitably my work will show my own interpretation. That's why if you want to alter what I write I should like to approve it first.'

'That sounds fair enough.'

Kit introduced Bert Matthews without saying precisely who he was. 'Now. What about photographs? Who does your printing and when do you want everything ready? I can either prepare copy with the photographs that I think should accompany the text or I can let you have all the photos and you can decide. I don't suppose you'll need more than twenty but I'll do a few more so you can choose.'

'The latter I think. Now what about payment?'

'You have already given me a retainer of £250. The remainder is due when I give you the final draft but I can wait until the first batch is printed. Any minor alterations will be done free of charge but if something happens and you need whole passages redone there will be an additional charge.'

Mr. Easton appeared concerned at this possibility. 'What can possibly go wrong?'

'Well,' replied Kit. 'Some of your cinemas may close or new places of interest may open.'

'I see. Well let's hope nothing like that happens after we've gone to press. Can I offer you coffee?'

'Thanks and I'll take your draft with me if it's handy.' Kit had already noticed the folder on the desk.

Coffee arrived and the business part of the meeting concluded, the conversation ranged far and wide. Kit enquired about any local history collection while Mr. Eastwood positively beamed when he explained that the library was right next door and it had an extensive local collection. 'I think you'll find them very helpful.'

'A letter of introduction from you would help,' explained Kit. Before they left a suitable letter was produced. The meeting had gone very smoothly and it was still only 11.30. No awkward silences and with everyone anxious to please each other. It had all been conducted in a friendly and businesslike manner. Bert was most impressed and said as much when they got outside. He declined Kit's offer to accompany him to the library, saying 'No. I've got a bit of business in town. I'll see you back in the car. What time?'

'Say 12.30. Then I'll treat you to a lunch somewhere in town,' replied Kit and with that they parted company.

In the library Kit produced his letter and was directed to the local collection. Whether it was the letter or his own friendly approach Kit could not be sure but the assistant couldn't have been more helpful. Usually on such research trips Kit had to do the fetching and carrying for himself. Here he had everything brought to him while the library assistant also offered suggestions of his own. In little under an hour he'd got the information he required on local follies, bygone and present day pleasure gardens as well as amusements, local activities and sports facilities.

He had also discovered many references to smugglers, grottos and caves. The bibliography was quite extensive and in spite of the many photocopies he had purchased he knew a return visit was essential. One thing really surprised him, namely the large numbers of royalty and other dignitaries who had visited the town as well as those who had embarked for the continent from or landed at Margate in the past.

Bert was waiting in the car and on hearing of Kit's successful research suggested they should drive out to The Captain Digby, a pub, right on the cliff top at Kingsgate and close to the mock Tudor castle. Instead of starting the engine Bert got out, motioned to Kit to move over to the driver's side and said, 'You drive. I'll give you directions.'

With what can only be described as a sheepish grin Kit needed no second bidding. After one false start they were on the move, Kit getting the feel of the car and appreciating for the first time how much higher from the ground the driver was in a Land Rover. The directions came quickly from Bert, 'Across Cecil Square, down Hawley Street and continue on this road up the hill past the bombed out church and keep on Northdown Road, the shopping area of Cliftonville.' The traffic was fairly light and in less than five minutes they were clear of the town and on to the narrow winding road to Kingsgate. Soon the large square castle came into view, perched perilously close to the cliff edge. Bert gave new instructions to slow down and turn left into the car park of the public house, The Captain Digby.

It was a popular watering hole and they were lucky to find a parking space. Kit showed off his driving skill by reversing neatly into one space with the car now facing the main door of the pub. Once inside Bert suggested they have either the ploughman's lunch or the cottage pie. They both chose the pie with cider to drink. As soon as they were seated Bert said, 'If you haven't managed to hire a car would you like to borrow the Land Rover?' Kit was surprised at this offer and pleased that Bert trusted him after such a short acquaintance.

'That really is most generous. I do need to go to the library again and over to the one at Ramsgate. I must also visit the places I intend to include in my piece. I'll be glad to accept. You must charge me the going rate.'

'That's O.K. then. We'll sort something out.'

They spent some time over lunch, chatting about the places Kit wanted to visit and Bert said, 'You do realise you're sitting in one of those follies at this very minute. There's a lookout tower a hundred yards away and of course there's the castle, the biggest fake of all.'

Kit had briefly discussed these with the librarian so was aware of their history and indeed the many false stories that were related to unwary visitors on mystery tours during the season. He appreciated there was much more to this region than he had originally thought.

'Bert, may I borrow the car this afternoon. I think I ought to make a start as soon as possible and this evening get down to the draft.'

'Yes. That will be all right. If I need transport I can borrow Beryl's little runabout.'

Kit wondered what Bert did for a living. Obviously The Haven took up a good deal of time during the tourist season but there must be more to occupy his time during the winter. For the moment he decided not to ask any direct questions and a few minutes later they returned to The Haven.

Kit went to his room for a wash and then had a quick look through his notes. The two main towns of Margate and Ramsgate and the smaller one of Broadstairs would be more than enough to complete his article. These together with the numerous villages on the Isle of Thanet would provide copy for several articles. The more he thought about it the more he became convinced that he should split the work into three parts for Capital News. Indeed it began to look as though there was enough material for a major book in spite of all those he had seen in the library collection.

He was about to set out in the Land Rover when Pauline arrived back from the station. He explained why he was driving her father's car and on the spur of the moment asked if she'd like to accompany him.

'Give me five minutes. I'd love to.'

She returned quite soon, having changed into very presentable slacks and an anorak. As she climbed into the passenger's seat Kit asked her to give the directions to reach Ramsgate library. The journey took only a few minutes along the main road then it was a question of following her precise instructions in the narrow streets to reach the library. It was a Carnegie building, having been presented to the town by that great benefactor, though somewhat hidden away in the back streets.

'I'll be here about two hours,' explained Kit. 'You're welcome to come with me or maybe you'd prefer to do some shopping,'

'I'll have a look round town and then I'll come and find you.'

Pauline disappeared into town and Kit went into the library. The collection here was not as large as at Margate but it was quite comprehensive and covered more of the area to the south and west, taking in Pegwell Bay and Sandwich. Whereas the sea had virtually left Margate harbour dry except at high tide. More money had been spent by the people of Ramsgate. They had built an inner harbour and an outer one. In fact with the yachting marina, both harbours and the terminal for off-loading new foreign cars it was a thriving port. Kit was interested in its history and needed to consult maps and guide books. Again the library people were most helpful and he was soon immersed in his research. He became aware of Pauline at his side and was surprised to find that it was almost 5 o'clock.

'Be honest,' she chided. 'You've forgotten all about me.

Kit felt himself beginning to redden and the blush on his face was answer enough for her accusation. He did have the grace to smile and said, 'If you had been here I would have been just as interested in you.' For the life of him he couldn't imagine why he uttered those words. To cover his confusion he said, 'I'll have to come back again. Could you give me five minutes to get to the end of this section.'

'Yes. That's all right. I'll wait outside.'

Returning his books to the assistant Kit expressed his thanks and asked if he could return the following day.

'Yes but this part of the library closes at 5.0 pm tomorrow.'

Outside kit apologised to Pauline for keeping her waiting. She assured him it was all right, adding that she appreciated how easy it was to lose track of time in libraries. 'Unless you're really disciplined you find yourself following all sorts of side tracks,' was her final comment.

'So what did you spend your money on?' Kit wanted to know.

'Oh nothing very exciting. The usual necessities. I spent some time down by the harbour. Dad has a couple of boats and a rather nice launch so whenever we visit Ramsgate we usually go down to see if everything is alright.'

'Nice for some.'

'Dad hires out the boats during the season and the launch too occasionally. That's his pet. It belonged to his father and a friend. When grandpa died his friend gave up his share to dad. So it really cost nothing although it does swallow up quite a lot in harbour dues.'

Now on the return journey, Kit felt himself wondering about Pauline. What did she do at the university? Did she work there? Was she a mature student and if so what was she studying? Had she been married and was now using her maiden name? She seemed happy enough and got on well with her parents. 'None of my business,' was his final thought as he stopped at the traffic light just before the turning into the road that took him back to her home. There had been more traffic on the return journey and the noise from the turbo charged engine had made it difficult to carry on a conversation.

As they got out of the car he said, 'Thanks for coming with me. It's nice to have company even if conversation is difficult. Maybe you could come again and help with the research. I'm sorry you had to wait for me.'

'I shall remind you of that from time to time. I did like the trip. Thanks.'

Chapter 4   Accidental Meeting

Most of Friday morning Kit spent sifting through the notes of his research and by lunch-time had produced an acceptable first draft of the Margate Publicity brochure. Later he borrowed the Land Rover and visited many places in Margate to take photographs that would complement the text of his article. His new camera was one of the new light weight models and he had plenty of spare film. He reckoned another full day's work would see the job completed. Two points struck him: the importance of Margate as a watering place in the previous two centuries and the number of libraries that once graced the town. One could still make out the various Georgian Squares that had once been so popular and there was still evidence of Tivoli Gardens and other places where the gentlefolk of the town went during summer evenings. During his brief visit to the library he had re-discovered details of travel in the 18th century. The roads from London were appalling so many people travelled down by sea. The wives stayed in the elegant houses, went for walks and visited the libraries. The husbands arrived by boat at the weekend. Indeed, humorous cartoons of the day depicted the husbands' boat arriving

Saturday turned out to be an eventful day although, on waking, Kit's only intention had been to continue the research for himself at Ramsgate. Pauline was on duty at the station buffet from 1.0 pm but she agreed to accompany him to Ramsgate and to help in checking references in the morning. Just before 9.0 o'clock they were on the way and soon after reaching Ramsgate he saw a sign directing him to the station. He mentioned to Pauline that he needed to get train times for his journey back to London so he might just as well get them now.

As he drew up outside the station he noticed a man getting down from a bus. He looked familiar as he walked quickly into the station. It was only a momentary glance and he might have dismissed it if he had not then seen two men who appeared to be following the first. They looked almost furtive in their efforts not to be noticed.

A thought struck Kit like a bolt from the blue. Surely it couldn't be the arsonist and the two CID men who had been trying to catch him for some time. He remembered the fleeting feeling of déjà vu when he saw the first man and realised there were some similarities to himself. They shared the same build, similar dark hair and facial features. Appreciating this he was relieved that the papers had retracted the photo-fit picture. Kit followed the two men into the station.

However, their quarry, if indeed he was that, had already disappeared towards the trains. Kit walked slowly to the enquiry desk, collected two small timetables and then returned to the car. He was about to get in when he glanced towards the station and saw an old man walking towards him with some difficulty. The man was intent on reading something and trying to keep his balance for he did not look up once.

Kit realised that for all the difference between this old man and the younger one he had seen enter the station they were one and the same. A chameleon indeed! Having decided that such was the case Kit waited for the other two to appear but they were nowhere to be seen. Kit wondered if they had been disposed of and then told himself to keep his imagination under control.

Pauline sensed that Kit had something on his mind and started to say something when Kit held up his hand. She now followed his glance and witnessed first hand the accident that happened. The old man, now very unsteady, stepped off the pavement just as a mini bus arrived to pick up a party of schoolgirls. There was no way the driver could avoid contact as the man virtually walked into the side of the bus. Kit was parked less than ten yards away and was with the man almost as soon as he hit the ground. In the few seconds before the man lapsed into unconsciousness there seemed to Kit recognition in his eyes and a feeble hand inviting Kit to take the man's wallet. Kit was more interested in the man's moustache that had come partly adrift so he pulled it off completely. In a single movement Kit pocketed the wallet and the moustache and called to Pauline to go to the station and telephone for an ambulance.

Pauline arrived with a blanket from the car before anyone else had moved. Then a few passers-by stopped and then the teacher in charge of the girls and finally the driver of the bus, somewhat shaken and complaining that it wasn't his fault. Kit asked them to move further back although a few continued to hover. The accident, like most others, happened in seconds and now they had to wait for the ambulance to arrive. It took only six minutes although it seemed much longer. Kit explained what had happened and the victim, while still in shock, was breathing more evenly. The ambulance man quickly checked the patient and within minutes he was transferred to the ambulance and was on his way to hospital when the police arrived.

Pauline and the other witnesses gave details to the police and soon the business of the station forecourt returned to normal. Kit suggested they continue to the library as planned and ring the hospital later to enquire after the man. He was about to get into the car when he noticed a plastic bag caught under the back wheel of the Range Rover. He bent down to remove it thinking it was empty but it obviously had a lot in it. He quickly covered it with the blanket and returned both to the back of the car before driving off. He realised it must have been the bag the old man was carrying and wondered if anyone else had noticed its disappearance and his retrieval of it. Kit reasoned that as the man obviously wanted him to take his wallet he might just as well look after the bag for him. The mystery began to deepen. The old man was not old and he no longer had a moustache for it was in Kit's pocket.

Trying to recall details of the accident he remembered that among the onlookers he felt sure he had seen the two men hovering in the background. He was also aware that by the time the police had arrived those two had left the scene. The research at the library went without incident. In spite of the delay, with Pauline's help he made up for lost time and she seemed happy to help. They left the library at 12.45, a little later than intended and Kit offered to take her directly to the station. She said it would be almost as quick if she returned home first and went on her bike. Then Kit asked her to find the hospital number to enquire about the patient.

As they were not relatives no information was forthcoming until she explained that she had called the ambulance that morning. They relented but only to say the patient was stable. There was little time left for her to talk to Kit as they had arrived home and she had to leave immediately.

After lunch Kit decided to carry on with the research so returned to Ramsgate and spent an hour tying up loose ends and obtained even more photocopies. Before leaving he sought out the assistant who had been so helpful and thanked her. Well it never did any harm to give thanks when due. Next he made a personal visit to the hospital to make enquiries about the traffic accident patient and was actually referred to the ward. Having introduced himself he was assured that the man was not seriously hurt and had in fact been discharged about half an hour ago. He had left with his sister who was going to look after him. Kit wondered about this turn of events and asked for the sister's address but hospital policy would not permit this so Kit decided on a little subterfuge. He explained that he had found the man's wallet at the scene of the accident. He sensed that the nurse was wavering and pressed home his advantage by saying if he returned the wallet the hospital need not bother any more.

The address was produced and Kit returned to the library to find out how to get there.

He spent some time actually looking for it but there appeared to be no house at the address. Locals whom he questioned had never seen it or knew the people who were supposed to live there. Two explanations were possible. He had either written it down wrongly or the hospital had made a mistake. He chose to believe the latter for where the house should have been there was nothing except weeds and wild flowers covering up the rubble of the house that had disappeared under a German bomb.

One other thing worried him. The victim's name he'd seen momentarily in the hospital record was different from that in the wallet. However sisters do change their name when they marry although he felt certain that whoever had taken away the patient it was not his sister. Once back at The Haven he resolved to take a closer look at the wallet and the contents of the plastic bag. Someone was not telling the truth. Kit smiled to himself at the thought as he, too, was not being entirely honest. At the garage Kit replaced the fuel he had used and as he got out of the car Beryl came to meet him. It seemed they were having a sort of high tea prior to seeing a play in Ramsgate. Would he like to join them for their meal and then accompany them to see *Time and the Conways* at The Granville Theatre. Kit replied that he would. 'That's very kind of you. You're treating me like one of the family.'

'That's settled then. We'll have tea as soon as Pauline gets home. The play starts at 7.30.'

There was almost an hour to kill so Kit went to his room and typed out the report to be sent to his editor. At this stage, not wishing to issue it under his own name he headed the piece *From our own correspondent*. Max would appreciate the need for secrecy and would get back to him if he needed further explanation. The gist of the report ran:

The police photo-fit given yesterday was an error and an apology has been published. A man was knocked down outside Ramsgate station today and was taken to Ramsgate hospital. He was not seriously injured and after a check-up was discharged into the care of his sister who lives locally. A police statement suggests no action will be taken against the driver of the bus as the victim was to blame for the accident. This is confirmed by several eye-witnesses. Two other men thought to be accompanying the victim disappeared before they *could be questioned.* 'That should put the cat among the pigeons,' reflected Kit after he had phoned in the report. Fortunately Max was not there so it was recorded and Kit hoped he would not return the phone call too soon. His own actions and thoughts had been too confusing for him to give Max a reasonable explanation.

Pauline arrived home and they sat down to their high tea, not in the restaurant but in the family dining room. Beryl said, 'I hope you like it. It's one of our favourite quick meals.'

'I'm sure I shall,' said Kit and meant it. It was macaroni cheese but with a difference. Tomatoes had been cut into small pieces and placed in the bottom of the dish followed by the usual macaroni cheese and the whole lightly grilled. It was accompanied by freshly baked bread and butter, a sustaining yet easily digested meal. This was followed by a trifle. Kit, who appreciated the effort that must have gone into making it, had never eaten a better macaroni cheese dish and enthusiastically complimented Beryl and asked if he could include it in the next edition of his book.

Bert drove them into Ramsgate and they were shown to their seats a few minutes before the curtain went up. The play, given by the local rep, was performed with competence and afterwards Bert drove them slowly towards the harbour. As they descended the long drive down towards the water, twinkling lights from the ships in the inner harbour were reflected in the water and cast a magical air about the place. Kit, thinking they were going to see the launch said he'd heard about Bert's pride and joy.

'We'll leave that for another time. Now we're going for a late supper. Is that alright with you?'

'Yes, of course. If this is how you live down here I'll have to come again.'

'Well it's not always like this. It just happens to be Beryl's birthday.'

A late night supper in a waterfront restaurant was the last thing Kit had expected when he'd agreed to join them. Forgotten for the moment were the various pieces of writing that had still to be finished. Put firmly to the back of his mind was the job of looking through the wallet and the bag and indeed the events following the accident and his visit to the hospital. This family was making him feel so welcome, almost treating him like one of the family that he felt a slight sense of guilt that he had told them the full purpose of his present contract with Capital News.

Bert and Beryl, it seemed were well known at the restaurant and once they had sat down the owner came over to welcome them. Kit was introduced and the waiter came over to take their order. There were several fish dishes but they all decided to have Dover sole with all the trimmings. While waiting for their meal to arrive there was the usual chatter, stories of the day's happenings being exchanged and general light-hearted conversation.

Pauline couldn't resist telling how Kit was so absorbed in his research that he'd completely forgotten all about her but the laughter that followed was good-natured. Kit excused himself and moved to the back of the restaurant, catching the waiter's eye. 'Could you bring a bottle of champagne towards the end of the meal. Here's my credit card.'

'Yes sir. Thank you.'

They all enjoyed the meal and Beryl was somewhat taken aback when the champagne arrived. 'It's my way of saying thank you to a lovely couple and to Pauline of course.'

'There you are Mum. I'm an afterthought again.' Pauline was smiling as she said it and everyone laughed. It was time to leave the restaurant. 'Who's driving?' enquired Bert. 'I'm not. That's for sure.'

'Nor me,' added Kit, 'And I don't think the birthday girl should on this special day.'

'That leaves you girl,' replied Bert, handing over the keys to his daughter.

She needed no second invitation and starting the car drove them the long way home. They went along by the harbour, up the winding Madeira Drive and along the top towards Broadstairs. She then turned inland for a while and then out towards the North Foreland lighthouse. Kit knew where he was now but instead of going along Northdown Road she drove along the coast road and ended up at Margate harbour and along to the clock tower before finally turning inland. The crisp night air finally woke them up and by the time they reached home they had all recovered from the effects of their evening meal and were chatting away.

'I did enjoy tonight,' said Kit. 'Thank you for inviting me. Happy birthday Beryl.'

The next morning in spite of the late night everyone was up quite early. During the morning the police arrived to question Bert, thinking he had been the driver of the car that had assisted the old man. Kit was summoned and explained again to two different policemen exactly what had happened. The police had apparently followed up the address given by the hospital and had found, like Kit, that it did not exist. He answered their questions as best he could but decided this was not the time to mention the bag although he did hand over the wallet. The police also wished to see Pauline who was able to confirm everything that Kit had told them.

As soon as the police had gone Kit excused himself saying he must write up some of his notes in order to earn a crust. The layout for his article finally began to take shape and at the end he thanked both libraries for their help. Sunday, traditionally a day of rest for him was proving to be anything but that. Having spent until midday on the article he began another report on the arson and the mystery man. Glancing over the story so far written and the update he now added the information he thought should keep the editor sweet for a couple of days. So far neither King nor Sutton, the other reporters, had put in an appearance and Kit began to feel that he was here on his own. There was nobody in the office when he phoned in his report, not that he really minded. He thought it a little strange, however, that Max had not got in touch with him as it had been he who had instigated this special assignment.

After lunch which he had with the family he asked them to help him for a few minutes. He gave them each a piece of paper with a name at the top and asked them not to reveal that name but to write a description of that person. Pauline described her mother. Bert pictured Pauline and Beryl described her husband. In fact they were all remarkably good likenesses. On a second sheet of paper he wrote the same name at the top of each, his own. This time there were similarities but also remarkable differences in the descriptions. Bert immediately realised the significance of this little experiment especially regarding the photo-fit picture, now withdrawn.

Kit then told them about his brief exchange with the injured man at the accident and then said. 'I believe there is a sinister plot afoot and I can't begin to understand what it's all about. At face value it seems that the man was up to no good and that the plain clothes men were following him. On the other hand the fact that he almost eluded them and that they have now disappeared could also mean that he was the good guy and the followers are not who they seem. There's one other point. When Pauline enquired about the victim she didn't really get a satisfactory answer. When I visited the man in hospital he had apparently been discharged.' He continued, 'I think he was spirited away, possibly against his will but he was certainly not at the address the hospital gave me. The police who called this morning didn't find him either. I suspect their orders came from high up and not the local constabulary. The reason I'm putting my thoughts into words is so that you are aware of what I think. We have something of a mystery. Can you think over what I've told you and let me know if anything else occurs to you.'

There was complete silence for almost a minute and then they all began talking at once. Kit interrupted their questions and asked them to keep everything within the family for the time being. They assured him they would and then got down to the business of question and answer. The afternoon passed quickly and it was time for a cup of tea. Kit decided to stay on for another week and Beryl agreed so he insisted on settling his bill to date. Kit planned to complete his article for the publicity department and take it down to them by Tuesday and spend some time following up any leads regarding the arson attacks although nothing new had been reported for two days.

The final two days he hoped to take as a holiday and spend it at Pegwell Bay and Sandwich before returning to London on the Monday. He asked Pauline to spend the last two days with him and was pleased when she agreed if she could get someone to stand in for her shift on Saturday morning. Kit spent most of Sunday evening going through the plastic bag. The family wanted to know what was in it but he said he didn't want to involve them at the moment. He couldn't explain, even to himself, why he had waited so long before checking the contents. Even now he felt a little reluctant to know what the bag contained not wishing to become involved in something over which he had no control.

The first thing he found was another wallet containing credit cards and a warrant card, claiming that the victim was a customs officer called Brian Chalmers. Two ten pound notes, three fives and a few coins were the only other things in this wallet. But the plastic bag contained much more. No wonder it was heavy. There were several maps covering the east coast from Cromer and down to Folkestone with a few special ones of river mouths and marinas. Even more significant were tide tables in the shape of Brown's Nautical Almanac. A small notebook contained many entries obviously in code but most of the bag was really a survival kit consisting of a woollen hat, plastic mac as well as a change of clothes. There were also several lengths of nylon rope and a large plastic sheet together with matches, a small stove and several metal skewers. Kit made a list of all that he found and replaced everything carefully back in the large bag.

Chapter 5   Cards on the Table

Kit showed the contents of the plastic bag to Bert soon after breakfast on Monday but asked him to keep the information to himself for the present until he had decided his next move. During the daylight hours of Monday and Tuesday he continued with visits to various places he wished to include in his forthcoming articles. The evenings were spent writing up his notes and adding his personal impressions. Sometimes he added an historical note about important individuals connected with the locations.

On Wednesday, a day later than he had intended, he rang Mr Eastwood to tell him the draft was ready and took it down straight away. He now felt freer to concentrate on his special assignment regarding the arson attacks on property in the local area and also to find out more about Brian Chalmers and the significance of the items in his plastic bag.

Kit tried various ways of breaking the code and suddenly realised it was not really a code at all but rather an accurate location of all the incidents that had occurred down the east coast, hence the need for all the maps. No dates were given but a series of eastings and northings gave the exact spot where the arsonists had been at work. A number in red followed each set of numbers so from 1 to 23 Kit was able to follow the track of the arsonists and Chalmers.

According to the papers the incident that had sent Kit down to Margate had happened last week and on the list was number 23. However, number 24 was not listed although Kit knew it had occurred and knew roughly where it was and also the reason for its omission. Chalmers did not have time to include it. Possibly he had recovered sufficiently to carry out another attack or was he, as the warrant suggested, a customs officer. Not being sufficiently versed in what customs officers really did Kit thought it possible that they may also have undercover officers as did so many services.

It was fast approaching the time when he should make contact with the authorities but which. The police, the coastguards or the customs were all important. Before deciding he would try to visit the most recent outbreak. In the Land Rover he headed towards Pegwell Bay, stopping a few hundred yards from the barn as reported in the paper. It was almost hidden from his sight by a screen of trees but through binoculars, borrowed from Bert, he could see it was still smouldering. The fire brigade was still in attendance, damping down and there were a couple of policemen to keep sightseers at bay. There was no way he could get closer without being observed.

Moving the binoculars to the south he took in the sweep of the bay and was surprised how wide it was especially with the tide out. He could just make out the water's edge and as the sun broke through he could see the river, a thin silvery ribbon to the north of Sandwich. He wondered how far the water came up the beach at high tide. Obviously it didn't matter for the hovercraft but for a number of boats flopped over on their sides it was a long way for the owners to reach their craft. Although now virtually high and dry the fact that there were so many suggested they were in regular use. Others were beached closer to the road that ran along the coast to Sandwich past the two cooling towers of the huge power station that dominated the skyline. Here, surely, was a suitable target if someone was intent on causing real problems.

Kit began to look forward to his weekend break, a mini holiday before he returned to London and got down to work once more. From his copious notes he had already singled out Sandwich as a fascinating place to explore with its long history going back to the time when Dutch weavers had arrived and even further back to when the Romans were in residence. His mind now made up he decided on a direct approach to the police guarding the dying embers and to play it by ear from then onwards. A few minutes later he stopped the car, got out and approached the two policemen. 'Anyone from the press been allowed here yet?' he enquired

'No. I think they've lost interest. There have been so many incidents,' replied one officer for which he received a warning glance from his older colleague.

'Any ideas how it happened and who did it?' continued Kit, anxious to set up a rapport but not wishing to appear too inquisitive.

'We suspect the same group who have been responsible for all the others. No idea how it started. The fire people might tell you. Are you a reporter?'

'Not exactly. I am a reporter but I'm not down here for this. I'm just gathering facts to entice more visitors here and just happen to be passing.'

'Can we see your press card?'

'Certainly,' replied Kit, producing it for the second time in a week.

'Tom. Take Mr Tynan over to the fire officer and see if he can tell him anything.'

'I'm much obliged. It'll be nice to get one over the regular reporters,' replied Kit, shaking hands with the older constable.

The fire officer put down his mug of tea and went through the usual preliminary questions with Kit. He was not able to tell him much more than was obvious. Attached to the barn was a small outhouse. Inside had been a table, a couple of chairs, a bed alongside one wall and a fireplace. There was even a sink with a cold water tap. The lock on the door had been forced and it seemed that a fire had been started by a tramp in order to keep warm. Somehow the fire had got out of control and had spread rapidly to the barn, burned through the wooden partition and set fire to the straw inside. The fire had also destroyed another room on the other side.

Further investigation had shown that firelighters had been used at strategic intervals to ensure that the fire spread rapidly. So the original story of the tramp starting the fire had been discarded in favour of the obvious arson. By the time the fire brigade had arrived all three buildings were well alight. Kit thanked the fireman and asked if he could mention his name. 'Use the information if you like but stick to the facts. I'd prefer it if you suggested you overheard me discussing it with the police.'

Kit, somewhat puzzled by this remark, nevertheless thanked him and left. His mind now made up, Kit went directly to the nearest Customs post, at the hoverport. He introduced himself to the duty officer, showed his press card and asked if he could see Mr Chalmers. 'No one here by that name sir,' was the quick reply. 'What's it in connection with?'

Kit felt like saying that if Mr Chalmers was not there he saw little point in continuing the conversation. Instead he refrained from such a direct rebuff. Kit had rehearsed his opening gambit and went on, 'Well it's a long story really. I've come across some documents that seem to belong to Brian Chalmers and I thought he was attached to this unit and I'd like to return them.'

'Well he's not here,' replied the man.

'Do you know him?' continued Kit.

'Not really. I've heard the name.'

Kit persevered. 'Who is the most senior officer on duty? Please give him this and ask him if he can spare me a few minutes.' With that Kit gave him a sealed envelope and the man disappeared. On a single sheet of paper inside the envelope Kit had written.

> BRIAN CHALMERS
> RAMSGATE STATION
> RAMSGATE HOSPITAL
> BUT NOT TR3555 6512 (24)

The messenger returned very soon and said, 'Please come this way,' and motioned him through a door and past two scanning devices that immediately detected Kit's camera and keys. Once these had been cleared he was allowed through and into the senior officer's sanctum.

'Please sit down Mr Tynan. I'm Ian Gregory. You took your time getting here.'

Afterwards, Kit was surprised at his own unhurried reply. 'Well I had to make sure I was coming to the right people and I had a few things to complete first. Now I'm here what can you tell me?'

'Let me pose the same question to you,' replied Gregory. 'What can you tell me?'

'Well for a start you can turn off that tape recorder,' said Kit, indicating the small machine on the table that was clearly recording.

'Someone said you were bright. Glad to oblige,' replied the customs chief and tuned off the machine.

'Who said I was bright?' demanded Kit and before you answer please turn off the recorder inside your desk.'

'My, my. We are suspicious.'

'So would you be if you knew how I came to be sitting in your office at this time. Incidentally I have left a note to be opened no later than two o'clock today telling people precisely where I am so we have a little over three hours and that includes lunch to conclude our business.' Kit registered the surprise on Gregory's face although inwardly he felt far from happy. Gregory opened the drawer and flicked a switch. Later, Kit was never sure if he had been too clever at the interview. For all he knew Gregory may have just switched the recorder on but it was a chance he had to take. In any case it didn't really matter. He was, he felt, catching on fast in this his first cat and mouse game.

Gregory now smiled. 'Time for coffee?'

'Yes please. Two sugars.'

'We'll talk for a while and then you can stay here for lunch if you like.'

'That's nice. Sorry I was awkward just now. It's been one of those weeks.'

'Perfectly understandable.'

'By the way, before we get started,' Kit interrupted. 'How is Brian Chalmers, if that really is his name?'

'He's almost fit. Got a bump on the head, from those two thugs he met at the station. We know a little about the incident. Please tell us more.'

Kit did just that, explaining that it was pure chance that he was at the station when it happened. Although he'd never met Chalmers he sensed a sort of recognition and when Chalmers had indicated for him to take the wallet he had done so automatically and then seeing the false moustache had come adrift he pocketed that also and then retrieved the plastic bag. Kit told Gregory what he was really doing in Thanet and then after the accident of his visit to the hospital. He explained that when he couldn't find the address he began to be suspicious, first of Chalmers and then of the two men.

'You know,' began Gregory, 'Brian had never seen you before but he thought he knew you, in fact thought you were one of us so he took a chance on handing over his wallet and the bag. How he managed to conceal the bag under your car he can't remember.'

Kit remained silent anticipating further revelations and they were not long in coming. 'You realise that you and Brian do look very similar. It was that which led him to believe you were also a customs officer because we had been told that someone at Dover resembled him.'

'Are you going to tell me more,' asked Kit.

'I think it's cards on the table for everyone. You first,' replied Gregory.

'Excuse me for a moment,' said Kit. 'I'll just go and collect his things from my car.' He returned to the Land Rover, retrieved the bag and quickly applied the false moustache and returned to Gregory's office. Gregory looked up as he entered but another man who was now in the office with him came forward to greet him, 'Hello Brian. I'm so glad you're up and about.' Moving forward, the newcomer realised his mistake at once. Kit smiled and held out his hand. The new man said, 'Ian was just telling me about you. I really didn't think you could be so like Brian. I'm Jim Terry by the way.'

'Oh,' said Kit. 'Glad to meet you'

Then Ian Gregory got down to business. 'You've obviously looked through the notes. Tell me what you know or what you think.'

'At first I didn't know who was the good guy and who were the bad ones. Once I'd identified the map references I thought Chalmers was definitely the bad one, then the entry that should have been there wasn't, that was the one near Pegwell Bay. I thought he might have been spirited away by the bad guys. He was certainly out of the picture therefore it couldn't have been him. It might still have been done by another bad guy. I really don't know what decided me.' Then with a silly grin on his face Kit continued, 'I suppose I thought anyone who looks like me can't really be bad.'

Jim Terry saw the funny side of that remark immediately. Ian Gregory took a second longer and then gave his side of the events. 'I must ask you to keep this to yourself and before we go any further I must ask you to sign a Declaration so that you will be bound by similar rules as us. You have somehow become involved in one of our problems and I think you should know something of what is going on. It could also be useful to us to have a reporter to provide press coverage we might need from time to time. You'll appreciate I need to approve anything you write otherwise it might jeopardise our operations.'

'Before you begin,' interrupted Kit, 'I do have to report to my newspaper. I'm quite happy for you to provide me with a cover story and I'll certainly let you see my copy before it goes to my editor but it must be as close to the truth as possible without causing problems to your people.' Kit read through the document he had just signed and handed it to Gregory. He realised he had little option but to agree if he was ever to glean any useful items that other reporters would not get their hands on.

Ian Gregory began, 'The whole business has been a muddle with the different authorities involved getting in the way of each other and the left hand not knowing what the right hand was doing. Our main interest is the smuggling that has seen a huge increase in recent years. It seems that the arson attacks were originally started by terrorists hoping to create panic to the general public. They obviously have their own agenda and I can't see that the arson attacks are in any way related to smuggling. The secret service informed the Foreign Office and they decided to let things drift. You know what a secretive lot they are so they didn't let the police or us know. Unfortunately things started to get out of hand as every firebug in the country decided to join in the fun. The emergency services were stretched to the limit answering calls, mostly hoaxes. At this stage the F.O. decided to let the rest of us know. Brian Chalmers, who was once based here had since become a field officer specialising in anti-smuggling work and for a time he was successful. Ultimately he was rumbled and ran into real trouble at Ramsgate when he was slightly injured. We managed to get him away from the hospital and he's recovering quite well'

'We suddenly realised we were no longer dealing with thieves and petty crooks but international gangs of the worst kind. For a price they will ferry in anything - drugs, diamonds, electronic devices and illegal immigrants. Some rival firms probably started the fires to destroy drugs if they couldn't pinch them. Or they could have been deliberately started to lure the police away from the actual place where they were operating. The Foreign Office is aware of this but there's little they can do without active support from across the channel. For the moment that is not forthcoming so we are very much on our own. Just this last week all our groups and all police forces have now been alerted so at least we are now pulling together. Any questions so far?'

'Just one. Why can't you ask for assistance from the Military Police. They're very sophisticated these days and any returning from Northern Ireland would find this a doddle.'

'The MOD is looking into this but apparently we shouldn't use military personnel for civilian problems. As far as I'm concerned any additional help would be welcome. I believe you are the first civilian to be involved and we need to keep quiet about it. After lunch I want to take you over to see Chief Inspector Simpson. He's the regional police chief. 'Let's go and have some lunch and you'll need to consider what I've told you.'

Lunch was a pleasant enough affair although Kit's mind was on other things. Gone for the moment were thoughts of his coming weekend break. He wondered what he had let himself in for. Maybe he would know by the end of the afternoon.

Chapter 6 Two Down

After lunch they set off for the police station in Ramsgate, Ian Gregory leading the way and Kit following in the Land Rover. The intention was to go directly to see the police but having gone less than half a mile Gregory pulled into the side of the road and got out. 'I've just had a call on our radio to go to our station at the harbour. It shouldn't take long but it' easier if I attend to it now.'

'That's OK. Carry on. I'll follow.'

A few minutes later they drew up outside the customs sheds and Gregory went inside to reappear a few moments later. They set off once more, retracing the first part of the route, moving slowly through the traffic and obstacles along the harbour. Out of the corner of his eye Kit caught sight of a figure he thought he recognised. Although only a glimpse he was sure it was one of the men who had attacked Brian Chalmers. He flashed his headlights at Gregory in the car ahead and both cars drew to a halt. Gregory was first out and came rushing back. For a man of his bulk he moved with remarkable ease.

'Problem?' queried Gregory.

'I hope I'm not seeing things,' replied Kit. 'I believe one of the men who attacked Chalmers has just gone into that chandlers,' indicating a harbour store about fifty yards behind.

'We'll take no chances. Thanks,' replied Gregory and returned to his car to make an urgent call on his radio. 'This is Ian Gregory. I'm at Ramsgate harbour outside Potters, the chandlers. Get in touch with Chief Inspector Simpsom and tell him we have a suspect inside. Ask him to lay on some men and approach quietly.'

'Yes sir,' came the response from Jim Terry. 'Shall I come over?'

'No thanks. It's really a police matter. I'll let them get on with it.'

Even as the radio clicked into silence the suspect came out of the store carrying a package and a jerrycan. The radio came alive again. 'This is Ian Gregory. Our quarry is on the move again. He might be putting out to sea. Ask the harbour master what boats are going out this afternoon. One more thing. Can you get on to the police. Tell them what we suspect and suggest it might be advisable if they came along.

Kit continued to keep the man under observation and watched him walk the length of the marina and out along the west pier of the Royal Harbour where he disappeared. He had just reported this to Gregory when the man reappeared retracing his steps and this time he had another man with him. They both entered the chandlers.

'It definitely looks as though they are on the move. If only we could be sure that's the right man. We can't go round stopping innocent people.'

'I guess not,' replied Kit. 'I'm pretty sure the second man is also the other one I saw at Ramsgate station. Surely there is someway we can stop them.'

'I'm afraid not. It's the price we have to pay for living in a democracy. The police have to let people commit a crime first before they can intervene. In this case I can't act at all. We have to wait for the police.'

The two men came out of the shop, carrying between them a long crate that appeared to contain a lot of equipment or supplies. It could have been quite legitimate stores but Kit was convinced it was guns and ammunition. He said as much to Ian Gregory, who smiled and urged Kit to keep his imagination in check. They watched as the suspects walked slowly along with their burden, taking their time to cover the two hundred yards along the top of the harbour. Although from their position the watchers couldn't actually see what was taking place it was fairly obvious that the stores were being lowered down to a boat. A movement behind attracted their attention and they realised that the chandlers was closing for the day. Gregory wrote down a hasty description of the man who left and soon after the police arrived in an unmarked car.

Gregory introduced Kit to the newcomers, an Inspector Robson, a sergeant and two constables. They had just exchanged news when a launch began to move slowly towards the harbour entrance. A lamp flashed from the harbour master's lookout and when this signal was ignored a loud hailer clearly ordered the launch to stop. Those on board either didn't hear or didn't care for its speed increased quite rapidly so that by the time it was clear of the harbour it was doing well over 20 knots and making for the open sea.

Gregory was on the radio again, urging that the lifeboat might be launched. He handed the phone to Inspector Robson asking him to use his powers of persuasion. He needed no second urging and was soon giving directions to the harbour master. 'The speed of the launch is probably 25 knots. The direction at present is 015 degrees. At this rate they'll be in France in little over half an hour.'

The launch changed direction and once clear of the long arm of the ferry terminal it moved through almost 90 degrees and was now heading south-west. This change was reported Gregory decided they could do no more at present and suggested that as it now looked as though the launch was heading for the shore or the river they might get a better view from Cliffsend at the edge of the town. One policeman remained in his car in case the chandlers opened again. Kit took one of the constables with him while the others went with Gregory. They drove westwards towards a slight rise in the ground and from their vantage point could see the whole sweep of Pegwell Bay and the approach to Sandwich.

The launch was heading towards the river mouth and Gregory was on the radio once again, this time to the coastguard. He wanted to know about the tides and whether there was sufficient water for the launch to travel over the Sandwich flats. Through his binoculars Kit could see quite clearly the channel made by the river as it snaked across the bay. He also realised that although the tide was coming in the depth of water on either side of the channel might not yet be enough for even a small motor boat.

Gregory smiled as he listened to the reply and relayed it to the others. It seemed that at this time of the year and this period of the tide the depth of water would not be sufficient. Moreover the wind was making the water quite choppy over the flats. The main channel was perfectly safe but if the men thought they were being followed they might be tempted to take a short cut over the shallow water

Those on board the launch seemed oblivious to the danger zone they had entered. They left the safety of the channel and cut across the mud flats looking for a shorter distance to the shore and hoping the tide had come in sufficiently to give them enough water below to keep them afloat.

Although the tide was coming in it was not fast enough and soon the inevitable happened. The launch ran out of water, slithered over the mud and came to a shuddering stop. The sensible thing would have been to wait for the tide to refloat them.

The two men on the launch had other ideas. They threw overboard a rubber dingy, got in it and began paddling furiously towards the shore. Because of its much smaller draught they may well have made it even though they had more than a mile to go. A third man appeared on the launch and called to them to stop. They would have none of it and continued to paddle towards the shore. The third man suddenly appeared on the launch again, this time with a rifle and aimed three shots at the dinghy and his aim was deadly accurate. Three holes appeared in the dinghy and each passing second it got lower in the water until most of the gas had escaped and it became stuck on a mud-bank.

When no further shots came in their direction the two fugitives attempted to wade ashore but quickly became stuck in the oozing river mud.

The weight of both men and the suction from the mud had a disastrous effect on them The chief decided to ask for help from the RAF. He explained the situation and wondered if they could possibly manage a rescue mission. He was advised that it would take at least twenty minutes. Kit, through his binoculars could see, even from that distance that the men were becoming weaker not only from shock and the cold but also from the sheer physical effort of trying to stay alive.

He tried not to waste too much sympathy on them but it was obviously an unpleasant way for anyone to die. The minutes ticked by and seemed to stretch into hours. Meanwhile, Gregory having seen their distress had radioed the lifeboat and wondered how close they could get to the men. A few minutes later they heard two maroons calling the lifeboat men to stations and in a remarkably short time the lifeboat appeared round the headland steering directly for the safety of the river channel. During all this time the tide had steadily been coming in and it seemed that most of the bay was covered with water. Kit looked at the launch but it appeared to be stuck fast. Shifting his gaze he saw that the men were also stuck fast and now a new menace threatened – the incoming tide, now swirling around their chests.

Soon, more or less on time, the heavy beat of the RAF helicopter blades could be heard. It became a race as to which would arrive first, the lifeboat or the RAF and even if either would be in time to save the men. The lifeboat slowed its approach and hailed the man on the launch. Kit thought it would go first to the men in the water but possibly there was not enough water for the boat to get close. A loud hailer came into use. 'Stand by. We are firing a line over you. Make it fast to your stern.' There was a puff of smoke and the line snaked out across the water separating the two boats. The practised aim of the crewman needed no second attempt as the line fell accurately over the launch. Quickly the unknown man secured it and the coxswain put his engine into reverse. Gradually the line tightened and took the strain. Slowly at first then faster the launch was quickly re-floated.

'Stand by,' came the call from the lifeboat. 'We'll give you a tow back to Ramsgate but first we need to see what happens here. What's your name?'

'I'm Roger Kemp, the owner of this launch. I don't know who those other two are.'

'Do you want to come aboard or stay there?'

'I'm OK. I'll stay here but thanks for the tow.'

The noise from the RAF machine drowned any further conversation. The rescue helicopter took station over the men with a crewman already suspended on a line and now very close to the men in the water. The RAF man managed to get a harness over one and gave the signal to be hauled up. The aircraft took the strain and gradually the man was hauled from what might have been his watery grave. The RAF man was lowered again and returned safely with the second man. All fight had gone from them and they were content to rest in the cabin, being attended by those on board as the helicopter made its way to the hospital at Ramsgate,

Kit suddenly realised that even though they had caught the suspects the time and effort involved had been enormous involving several different organisations. At least this part of the operation was over and the various services were able to stand down awaiting their next mercy call. Gregory was informed of the outcome and in particular the identity of the third man. He was an innocent bystander who had been on his launch making it ready for the winter. He had been overpowered and put in the toilet that was then wedged shut. He had only made his escape once the boat had hit the sandbank, possibly the wedge having been dislodged by the impact.

On reaching the deck he had at once taken in the situation and using one of the rifles the man had taken on board had deliberately punctured his own dinghy. All this was confirmed when they got to Ramsgate and met up with the police again. Inspector Robson thought they might gloss over the use of the rifle by someone who did actually possess a firearm certificate although not for its most recent use. The policeman turned to Kit and said, 'Nice work, Mr Tynan. I think you've earned your stripes today. Even so I think we'd better continue to the police station and meet the chief as originally planned. Please follow in your car and as soon as we've finished you'll be glad to get back to The Haven.'

The short distance to the police station was accomplished without further incident and when they had been ushered into the chief's office Gregory opened the conversation. 'Sorry we're a couple of hours adrift but we think we've managed to catch a couple of villains for you.'

'Hello Ian. It's nice to see you again. Two down. I wonder how many more there are. I followed most of it on the radio. Congratulations to you all and especially to you, Mr Tynan. It's nice to have you on our side. I think we may have met before.'

Kit looked with renewed interest at the police chief and cast his mind back to when he might have been in trouble with the police. Simpson looked intently at Kit for any sign of recognition but there was none.

'You've noticed the likeness too?' interjected Gregory

'No it's not that although he is similar to poor old Brian but I'm sure Mr Tynan and I were at school together.' Turning to Kit he enquired, 'Did you go to Hereford College and win the major literary prize two years running?'

'Well, yes. That's a long time ago.'

Kit retraced his school-day memories in a matter of seconds and as the years rolled away the name of Simpson came to him although he could not place the face that now confronted him. He made a gallant effort.

'Sorry. I didn't recognize you at once. The name was familiar but I couldn't place your face. I'm glad you've done so well. It's a small world.'

At ease now and with the introduction formalities completed George Simpson remarked, 'I see no reason why we shouldn't let Mr Tynan in on most of what we know.'

'Before you say anything,' interrupted Kit, 'I must tell you that although I'm down here to research some articles on Thanet my editor also asked me to keep an eye out for this arson problem. He expects me to report something.' Kit went on to explain how he had been persuaded and brought out for the first time the special document that Howard Marshall had given him.

'What an honest chap you are,' smiled the policeman. 'It's very naughty of your editor to keep you in the dark but on the other hand he didn't want you to go looking for trouble. This document is a special clearance and although you don't know it you have been vetted by Special Branch in case you were arrested.'

Kit felt relieved and then angry that Marshall had not taken him completely into his confidence. 'My own editor is a personal friend but I hardly know Marshall. I shall not forget this in a hurry.'

'Think nothing more about it,' suggested Simpson. 'You need to file your report and I'll approve it. Please don't give the names of the villains and not too many details. It would be in order for you to say that a reporter on Capital News was instrumental in assisting the police in the arrest.'

'Thanks. There's just one more thing,' added Kit. 'You probably know that I'm staying at The Haven. In fact the car I'm driving belongs to Mr Matthews. They obviously know something of my involvement. May I tell them about the events this afternoon?'

'Yes. That will be alright but they must keep it to themselves. We know Bert Matthews very well. He's absolutely to be trusted. Perhaps when he knows you a little better he'll tell you why we regard him in such high esteem. That's all I can say at present.'

Kit tried to get more information but George Simpson was adamant. 'I'm glad we've met after so long. Although we were not close at school it's always nice to meet old school chums. Call on me whenever you like. With a bit of luck our current problems will move on to someone else's patch. It may be necessary to ask you to identify these two characters later on but we'll try and keep you out of it. Never know. We may be able to use you again. Thanks.'

Kit felt he was being dismissed. A handshake from the policeman and a cheery goodbye from Ian Gregory and Kit was free to return to the relative calmness of The Haven. So much had happened today, most of it unexpected. The two arrests had been accomplished more by luck than anything else. It was still only Wednesday. It was early closing again and he had been in Thanet for just eight days.

One major thought puzzled him. In spite of Brian Gregory's theory Kit began to wonder if the arson incidents along the east coast might be connected after all and if so who was behind the organization. Each incident must involve at least one person and possibly more. If the purpose was merely to lure the authorities away from somewhere else the whole operation could be huge – and for what purpose. He felt quite sure the police and customs people had not given him the complete picture.

Chapter 7 Weekend Break

So much had happened in the eight days since Kit had first arrived in Margate and in spite of the unexpected events he had actually accomplished most of what he had planned. His articles for Capital News were now completed. The main purpose of his visit, the copy for the Publicity Department, had also been handed in. Moreover he had got closer to the arsonists than any of his colleagues. He had forgotten his anger towards Marshall and decided to say nothing about it when he returned to London.

On Thursday he telephoned Chief Inspector Simpson to say he had written a report for him regarding his involvement with the prisoners. In fact he had composed two accounts, the first a short report of 1500 words for his editor. The second, a more detailed account of all that had occurred since getting off the train eight days ago ran to 3000 words on six pages. He handed them to Simpson and waited while the policeman read every word and then passed them over to a colleague.

When he had finished Simpson turned to Kit. 'I'm impressed with the detail in this larger report, even the time when the events took place. Has Ian seen it?'

'No. Perhaps you could send him a photocopy. This one is really for your files. Although I don't expect to be present at any other of your arrests I thought you'd like this as a souvenir.'

'Marvellous. If you don't mind I'll just add the names of the officers involved and then file it as it is. Thanks very much.' Kit made no effort to leave so Simpson asked, 'Is there something else?'

'You mentioned yesterday that you knew Bert Matthews very well. I haven't given him details of what happened yesterday and only the bare bones of what happened earlier. I'd like to be able to tell him a little more. The second thing is can you tell me more about Bert and how you come to know him?'

The policeman settled back in his chair. 'First you can let him see the account you are sending to your editor. The other report is technically police property even though you wrote it. Second. Bert is something of a hero though few people know about it. He was one of the special Home Guard personnel during the war. One night, while on guard duty at Palm Bay he actually rescued a German airman whose plane had been shot down. He scrambled over the rocks and brought back this injured man though other members of the crew perished. On another occasion a German pilot landed his 109 in broad daylight because he'd run out of fuel and was attempting to set fire to it and escape into a small copse near his home and Bert took him prisoner. After the war he was for a time a special constable and he occasionally comes to one of our dinners. That's where I met him. When you see him you can tell him that I've told you and he may care to enlarge upon it.'

Kit thanked the police chief and left. He returned to The Haven and phoned in his report. Max was still away or was not taking any calls so Kit spoke to Maggie, one of the girls in the editorial office. After lunch he returned to his room and fell fast asleep on the bed. The events of the past few days had finally caught up with him or maybe it was the bracing Margate air he'd read about in last year's brochure. He reckoned he could manage a couple of days over the weekend for a break although he would definitely need to return to London on Monday. A glance through his diary reminded him of more appointments in Southend on Tuesday and Clacton on Friday.

He had asked Pauline earlier if she would like to accompany him on a visit to Sandwich. She had managed to get someone to do her shift at the station buffet so on Saturday after a leisurely breakfast they set out in the Land Rover, taking with them a picnic lunch prepared by Pauline. On the way to Sandwich they passed the replica long boat that a few years earlier had actually sailed across the North Sea, following the route of Vikings many years ago. Pauline gave a running commentary as they passed by and pointed out the nearby cross of St Augustine, the site of his landing in 983 and then just before they entered Sandwich they could see in the distance the old Roman fort of Rutupiae, known by its British name of Richborough Castle.

They drove directly into the ancient town of Sandwich and on Pauline's advice turned left immediately after crossing the river and parked by the quayside. The tide was in and the river was quite full. Kit, seeing this for the first time, asked Pauline if it would be possible to cruise up the river. It seemed that the Matthews family had done this several times but had never gone more than a few miles beyond Sandwich.

'If you feel like stretching your legs we could walk to the coast from here and have a picnic on the beach.' Pauline interrupted his thoughts and Kit was happy to go along with her suggestion. 'That's fine with me. You lead the way.'

They set off sharing the picnic things between them. At a leisurely pace they soon reached the sand dunes and then they were at the wide expanse of the open beach and Kit could see the channel stretching away in the distance. The beach itself was deserted and Kit was aware of just how easy it might be for anyone to land on these shores. Finding a sheltered spot among the dunes they settled down for coffee from the flasks they had brought. A few ships moving slowly in the channel gave little evidence of the huge amount of shipping that used the waterway.

Kit decided to tell Pauline a little about his recent interview with the police. She listened quietly with no interruptions until he had finished. He was glad he had unburdened himself but then felt concern in case Pauline might become a target for those causing the problems. 'What are you going to do?,' she wanted to know.

'I'm not sure. I'm not trained in these cloak and dagger activities so it's a question of being alert to anything unusual and letting the authorities get on with it. In any case I'm returning to London on Monday so I'll not be involved any more.'

'What can I say,' replied Pauline. 'You've had an exciting week and thanks for telling me. I'll keep it to myself and I'm glad we met. It seems a long time ago now.'

'Thanks for listening. I needed to get it off my chest. I reckon the arson attacks in other parts of the country and those here are not connected although the police think they are. I'll tell your dad this evening.'

'So we are going back this evening?' queried Pauline a slight smile on her lips.

Kit wasn't sure if it was a question or a statement or whether it required an answer. He decided to ignore it and began to collect the cups and biscuit wrappers from their coffee break. Pauline made no further comment so he thought he had misheard her remark. They walked southwards along the coast, past the golf course and then turned inland towards the town. Although not yet mid-day they decided to have an early lunch and found an ideal spot out of the wind in a local park. The weather in September can be unpredictable. Today they were lucky. The sun shone, the lunch was appetizing and washed down with a bottle of wine that Beryl had put in the basket. During a lull in the conversation Kit drifted off into a long sleep.

When Pauline gently nudged him awake he knew it had only been a dream yet the details had been so real and connected with his recent forays with the police. He dreamed he saw two more fire raisers and followed them as they walked slowly towards the quayside where he had left the Land Rover. The two villains entered the timber yard nearby and although there were several people around they proceeded to pour petrol over the timber and set light to it. In little more than a minute the whole place was enveloped in flames with dense black smoke rising high into the sky.

The arsonists came out of the gates, grinned to everyone and threw two bags of fireworks into the inferno. Soon, as well as the cracks and bangs of the fireworks going off everything was covered with specks of burning material including Bert's car. The two culprits stood watching their destruction for a minute or two and then calmly walked away. Kit stood rooted to the spot, unable to stop the fire or apprehend the men. Someone must have alerted the fire brigade for there could be no ignoring its clanging bell as it raced to the scene.

Kit awoke suddenly. Pauline leaned over and asked quietly, 'Enjoy your sleep?'

'Sorry. I must have been more tired than I thought or it was the wine. Is there a fire somewhere? I've just had a most vivid dream.'

As he spoke a fire engine raced as quickly as it dared through the narrow streets of Sandwich, its bell clanging urgently. Pauline suggested they should go back to the car, leave the picnic things there and look in at the town museum and then if there was time they could visit the Roman fort on their way home. The bell on the fire engine ceased as they walked towards the car park and Kit could scarcely believe his eyes when they reached the timber yard.

A small fire had burned a hole in the fence and caught some of the timber. It had been quickly extinguished and the firemen were now preparing to leave. For the moment Kit said nothing about his dream. The museum was shut and would not open again until next spring so they went into a tea-shop and Kit told Pauline about his dream. 'I dreamed I saw those two men we caught at Pegwell Bay. They deliberately set fire to the timber yard.' Kit told her the remainder of his dream.

Pauline interrupted, 'And then you woke up.'

'Yes.'

'Well you know, they say dreams happen in an instant. You probably heard the fire engine, had your dream and then woke up.'

'Now I'm disappointed. I thought maybe I was developing a sixth sense.'

The tea refreshed them and they made their way to the ruins of the Roman fort. There was time for a quick look round and they spent longer in the museum and shop although Kit had decided he would make an extended visit as soon as possible. In the meantime he bought a few postcards and a guide-book. They had a last look at the impressive ruins, this time noticing how close the river came to the outer ramparts and then it was time to return to The Haven for an evening meal.

The return to her home was almost in silence, each absorbed with their own thoughts but quite content. Kit was no longer a guest and joined the family for their meal and Beryl wanted to know all about their day out. After dinner Kit excused himself, saying he needed to make a few notes about the Roman fort and later that evening asked Bert about his wartime experiences and wondered if he would like Kit to write them up as an article for the local paper.

Bert seemed quite happy to talk about the war years and his time with the Home Guard which he explained was actually with the secret army. He explained about their hideouts, special training and weapons. 'Thank God we never had to put into practice any of the stuff we'd learned.' At the end Kit realised that he had learned very little of what went on in those dark days of World War II and concluded that Bert had been very clever in telling him so little. As for an article in the local paper Bert thought it had been so long ago it was best forgotten.

Sunday morning was bright and sunny so after breakfast Kit and Pauline set off again with a packed lunch. Kit tentatively enquired if Bert and Beryl would like to accompany them and was relieved when they both declined. Although little of the Roman fort remained it was easy to visualise that it had been a massive structure and military outpost that guarded the Wantsum Channel and saved a long voyage round the Isle of Thanet. It was difficult to appreciate that the very narrow river that now flowed past the fort had in Roman times been four miles wide.

Kit was also keen to find out just how far the present river was navigable and if indeed Thanet was still an island. They had their lunch in the grounds of the fort and had another look round the museum. On the way back to Margate Kit stopped at the café in Pegwell Bay and bought a couple of ice creams that they ate sitting on a wall overlooking the bay. Everything was peaceful with the tide just coming in. Kit looked out to sea and remembered the scene a few days ago when he had seen the men rescued from their potentially watery grave. As they got back to the car Kit handed the keys to Pauline. 'Would you like to drive a tired old man home?'

'Yes thanks,' she replied and as they settled into the seats she leaned across and kissed him lightly on the cheek. Thanks for today. I did enjoy it.'

Chapter 8   Return to London

Early on Monday morning Kit took his leave of the Matthews' household. Bert drove him to the station where he just had time to say goodbye to Pauline before the train whisked him back to London. They kissed briefly and he promised to keep in touch.

In spite of the hectic past few days it took little time for him to get back into his normal routine in the familiar surroundings of the city. On Tuesday morning he was summoned for a short conference with the editors to review all that had happened at Ramsgate. With evidence gathered from other arson attacks it was considered that very few of them could be traced back to subversive activists and that those down the east coast were not likely to be connected in any way to those in the south east. The fact that all the incidents had taken place on government land or buildings suggested that they could be down to someone with a grudge against the government. In fact two incidents in Lowestoft had proved to be the work of a certain Jeremy Essex who had been dismissed from his job in a bonded warehouse for theft.

Max decided that little would be gained from printing Kit's account. 'We'll keep this on file but at the moment it's a dead duck,' was his final comment.

Soon after lunch Kit was off again, this time in his own car, to visit a couple of towns in Suffolk. Having been in that area a number of times he made for his favourite hotel in Saxmundham and once settled in, his thoughts turned to Pauline. In the evening he rang her at home and they spoke for a few minutes. She seemed pleased that he had rung, reminded him that she would soon be returning to university but that he could always write to her there or ring her at the weekend when she usually returned home.

The next few days saw his new series of articles taking shape and he even managed to add a new recipe to be included in the next compilation of Katie Kooks. It was interesting work, delving into the past and relating present day situations to events in earlier times. New roads and bypasses around busy villages always seemed to uncover evidence of earlier civilizations. Although no expert in such matters Kit had acquired a superficial knowledge of bygone England. He was aware that not all of the anecdotes contained in his articles were true though they made interesting reading.

He had proved for himself that certain episodes in British history that he had learned at school were far from true. He had discussed his theories with an eminent historian who had agreed that in the telling and retelling of events some stories had been glossed over and important facts ignored or even altered to tie in with political thinking of the day. In time completely wrong facts had been accepted as true and even repeated. If ever he got the time Kit would like to study history and come up with some real life stories of earlier years.

Somehow the excitement of the recent days in Thanet kept coming to the surface and he wished for something exciting to happen now – not too exciting but with an element of surprise to keep him on his toes. These flights of fancy did not last long and he soon got down to the work in hand. He enjoyed his work and after all it provided a reasonable living and more or less at his own pace.

Saxmundham on the A12 had more or less kept its old world charm. Within easy reach of the capital, served by rail and road it was not too far from the coast and for those who wished for it there was safe sailing on the River Alde before it entered the North Sea. With so many leisure activities now available it seemed that this whole region was given over to fishing, sailing and adventure holidays. Writing about these and similar areas had provided Kit with a steady income either on contract or as a freelance journalist. He had established a good reputation and his articles were usually accepted.

In recent years he had tried his hand at short walking tours. Although these had been done many times before, his editor liked his easy-going style, the directions he provided, the line drawings and maps that accompanied his articles. One local paper had asked permission to gather together about a dozen into a small booklet. It involved little additional work for Kit and towards the end of the season he received a useful royalty.

Kit decided to walk a few local routes before the bad weather set in. So with camera and a small rucksack he set off. This time he hoped to stay somewhere overnight along the route. On such trips he usually started out about 8.30 and walked at a steady pace until 10.30 when he had a break for coffee from his flask. Notes were made along the way to indicate the route including anything of interest and an indication if permission was necessary to cross any field. The stop for lunch was usually at one o'clock, either eating a packed lunch or stopping at a pub before continuing the afternoon session.

Usually by 4.0 in the afternoon Kit began to look for somewhere to stay for the night. If he was unsuccessful at a pub there were usually local farms or even private houses that did bed and breakfast. He was always careful to introduce himself and tell people what he was doing and so far had been successful in receiving no rejections. Many people even in isolated houses usually welcomed the extra money a few walkers might provide. This time he mapped out a two day walk covering about 30 miles, managed to shoot some interesting photographs that he would later transfer as line drawings for greater clarity. He called in at the county library to confirm historical events of the area and this time stayed longer than he had originally intended.

A week later he returned to his home in London and checked his mail. The inevitable junk mail was thrown away, other letters quickly answered or filed for future attention and he was left with a letter from the police at Ramsgate thanking him for his assistance in recent events and asking him if he could attend a court hearing when it could be arranged. He rang them, confirmed that he would be available but would welcome a few days' advance notice.

That evening Kit had a phone call from Brian asking if he'd like to go sailing at the weekend. This meant going to Whitstable Friday afternoon, staying there overnight before getting the boat ready to sail to Ramsgate before laying it up for the winter. Brian was using the last few days of his leave before going back to work and Kit readily agreed to accompany him.

So on Friday afternoon, ahead of the general exodus from London, Kit travelled down the M2 and then on to the A299 just past Faversham and reached Whitstable just after 5 o'clock. Here was another old world town that had grown considerably in recent years. Kit called in at the estate agents next to the railway station and asked for one of their maps of the area. They were keen to show him a list of houses for sale but he declined saying he'd like to look around first. As he left he saw Brian coming out of the station and walked over to him. 'Can I offer you a lift, I'm going your way.'

'What a good idea,' replied Brian. 'I've a friend coming down for the weekend and I don't want to keep him waiting. I've actually left my car at Ramsgate so that if we manage to get the boat there tomorrow we'll have transport back here whatever the time is. Come and meet mother. I expect she's put on a good spread or we could go out for a meal.'

During the short drive to Brian's home the usual enquiries about each other's health revealed that all was well and spoke briefly about the forthcoming trial. The Chalmers house was situated on rising ground above the small harbour in the old part of the town. The main rooms faced west and caught the setting sun while it was protected from the north and east winds by a belt of poplars, their leaves gently shimmering in the slight breeze.

Mrs Chalmers greeted her son with relief and thanked Kit for looking after him. She knew about Brian's plans for the weekend and suggested they go out for a meal this time but that she would cook something special when they returned from Ramsgate. So after the traditional cup of tea as a welcome and a brief tour round the house and garden they walked down to a harbour restaurant for their evening meal. Brian opened the conversation. 'As we're in Whitstable we should have oysters but I can't stand them. We are happy for you to have them and I'm told this is the best place in town.'

'I'm sorry,' replied Kit. 'I've never tried them and if you don't mind I'll give them a miss too. I'm not a bad sailor but I don't want to temp my stomach.'

They settled on sea bream with all the trimmings, followed by a light egg custard and cheese and biscuits. By the time they had finished their meal it was dark outside. The clouds had disappeared and the almost full moon bathed the whole area in a soft light though dark shadows were cast where the moon shone against buildings. It was a magical scene, the twinkling lights of the harbour reflected in the water while out to sea they could just make out a few lights from nearby Sheppey.

When they reached home Mrs Chalmers retired for the night but Kit and Brian sat up a bit longer discussing the coming trip to Ramsgate. Then they too went to bed to a sound sleep, too far from the shore to hear the tide coming in yet lulled to sleep by the breeze gently blowing though the poplars at the edge of the garden.

The following morning they were up early. 'We'll have a full breakfast,' Brian declared, 'to keep us going and I've always found that a full belly is best to ward off any sea sickness.'

'The sea looks calm enough,' replied Kit. 'Do you think it's going to get rough?'

'Not really. We're a bit sheltered here but you'll be surprised how the sea changes. It can get quite choppy when we lose the shelter from the mainland. Don't worry. We'll be up on deck most of the time doing something.'

They said cheerio to Mrs Chalmers and walked down to the boat. By 8.30 they had cast off and Brian steered north for a couple of miles using the auxiliary engine. Once out in the channel between the mainland and the eastern end of Sheppey he instructed Kit in the art of unfurling and setting the sails. 'This is not really a racing yacht although when correctly trimmed we can get a good speed. I'll take the wheel for a while and you can watch and then you can take over, get the feel of the boat as she goes.'

For the next two hours Kit followed Brian's instructions and made sure he passed well clear of the buoys that marked a number of wrecks. 'Keep to this course. Watch out for other boats and don't let the bow go under the waves. When we clear the shelter of Southend we'll get the full force from the North Sea. I'm just going below to make us a hot drink.' With that Brian disappeared below and Kit was in charge for the first time of a small sailing boat though comforted with the knowledge that he was not really alone.

Nothing went wrong and in a few minutes Brian appeared with two mugs of hot Bovril. The sea was getting choppy with spray coming over the bow from time to time so that Kit's borrowed oilskins were wet. Brian handed one mug to Kit and then stood beside him. Not a word was spoken as they sipped their drinks but a nod of approval from Brian assured him that all was well. Just ahead and slightly to starboard the pier at Herne Bay came into view.

Brian handed him a pair of binoculars. 'Take a look. Not many people on the beach. See how rough the waves are breaking on the shore. We'll carry on past Herne Bay and in another four miles we'll be level with Reculver and four more miles it will be Birchington. All told we have 28 miles to go though with the tides it will be more like 35 that we have to cover. We'll have a midday meal just off Margate and with luck should reach Ramsgate by about four o'clock. That should give us time to get berthed before the light goes.'

Lunch was a hurried though sustaining meal of stew with slices of potatoes and vegetables all in one deep dish with the remainder of the liquid soaked up with large chunks of bread. This was followed by a tin of peaches shared between them. 'Once we get past the North Foreland we'll be running with the wind so we'll need to take in a bit of sail and before we enter Ramsgate harbour we'll take the other sail down and run in using the engine.' Brian was keen to show off his newly acquired boat but it was obvious that he handled it with accustomed ease.

Even with the brief instructions he had been given on this short voyage Kit felt he had learned more than could have been gained by attending several classes as he had been intending to for so many years. He was impressed by the safety equipment on board and when Brian introduced him to the small but efficient navigation equipment he was fascinated by it's accuracy. Even so it was essential to read charts accurately and to avoid the many sandbanks, shoals and war-time wrecks that still cluttered this part of the coast.

Brian flicked a couple of switches and spoke to the coastguards at North Foreland and got a weather report including the state of the tide at Ramsgate. His next call was to the harbour master at Ramsgate telling him of his ETA and requesting entry to the inner basin.

They were soon moored alongside the harbour wall with fenders over the side. This was the longest voyage Kit had made in such a small boat and he was surprised when once he had reached solid ground that he was a little unsteady on his feet. Brian smiled and assured him that it would soon pass. They made their way towards the town and stopped at the first phone box while Brian made a phone call. Kit thought it might be to his mother to let her know he had arrived safely but Brian told him, 'I've just rung Mrs Stevens and told her we'll bring the boat round to her yard tomorrow. She'll give the boat a thorough check, including the engine.'

Chapter 9 Learning about Boats and Justice

As they walked towards the shops Kit remarked, 'Must be an expensive hobby, messing about in boats.'

'Well I suppose it is but it's my only real extravagance and I intend to enjoy it while I can. Mrs Stevens runs a small boatyard. They used to build small boats but since her husband died they concentrate on repairs. You'll like her. Her husband used to be in the lifeboat crew until he was lost at sea. So now she's the figurehead and has retained all her old team. By the way, she has invited me to dinner and she insisted that I bring you along. Hope you don't mind.'

'No, of course not but I'm a bit scruffy.'

'She'll accept that but if you like we could go into town and buy something.'

'It'll be good to stretch my legs and an extra shirt always comes in handy so let's do that and I'll get a bottle of wine.' Kit made his decision and the thought crossed his mind that this was not the first time that Brian had been invited to dinner. Less than half an hour later they were back on the boat. Washed and changed, they walked towards the boatyard both looked quite presentable. Brian explained, 'We'll go there first and if she's already left we'll walk up the steps to her home. She doesn't exactly live over the yard but in a house at the top of the cliff.'

The wind that had blown quite strongly during the day had died away. The clouds had also gone and Brian said there would be a couple of days of fine weather.

Mrs Stevens had already left and Brian chatted to the foreman and explained that he was bringing the boat round tomorrow. 'That's OK. Well pull her up here first and check the hull and the keel. Does it retract?'

'Oh yes. I need to know that it's watertight. The previous owner said it was but it's best to make sure'.

'Absolutely. I gather from the boss that there is no real hurry as you don't need it till next spring. However if we finish it quickly do you want us to keep it here or moor it in the harbour.

'Not sure about that. I'll talk to Mrs Stevens tomorrow. Cheerio.'

And with that Kit and Brian began the long ascent of the steps that led to Mrs Stevens' home. A smiling woman of about 40 opened the door to their ring and said, 'Come in. I'm Georgina. You must be Brian and I assume you are Mr Tynan.'

'That's right,' agreed Brian. 'This is Kit or Christopher. I didn't realise that Stella had a daughter.'

'Well she does tend to keep me hidden. We just happen to be down here visiting. Come through. Mum's in the kitchen but we'll go into the lounge and have a drink. Let me take your rain coats.'

When Stella appeared she was a slightly older version of her daughter. She welcomed both her guests with a smile and a warm handshake for Kit. She kissed Brian lightly on the lips and remarked, 'Well, you don't look too bad after your brush with villains but it must have been a bit of a shock.' He merely nodded his head in Kit's direction and said, 'This is the chap I'm really grateful for being on hand at the time. We'll just have to wait and see what the judge has to say.'

'I'm relieved. Dinner will be about twenty minutes. I've just come in for a quick sherry.' Turning to Kit she raised her glass and said, 'Cheers. I hope your voyage wasn't too rough today. I'm dying to have a look at the new boat, Brian.'

'It was my first trip in a yacht and I quite enjoyed it but I don't think I can afford one just yet.' Kit was about to say more but stopped.

An alarm sounded in the kitchen and Stella made her excuses as she went to watch over the last minute preparations for dinner. Then Georgina took charge and ushered her guests into the dining room. There, with the curtains drawn back the large picture window looked out over the English Channel and on to the lights in the harbour. The meal was expertly cooked, each course being cleared away by Georgina into the kitchen while Stella regaled her guests with stories about boats she had recently repaired and their owners. A rich desert wine followed the last course and then Stella said, 'We'll go out onto the balcony for coffee and I've got a liqueur I'd like you to try. It's Van der Hum from South Africa made from oranges.'

They sat drinking and talking for half an hour. Brian suggested they help with the washing up but Stella said her guests were not invited to do the chores. Georgina volunteered and went to the kitchen. After a short while Kit excused himself and made his way to the kitchen. 'I couldn't let you do this all on your own so I've come to help. I felt I was intruding.'

'Oh, that's alright. They're old friends. I keep trying to get mum to marry again, preferably someone like Brian but I think she's too set in her ways.'

Kit didn't feel he could comment but asked her if she had any children. 'Yes. I have two. One of each. They're at home with my husband at the moment although we all come down as a family for our holidays. He's a Don at Oxford.'

So within a few brief minutes Kit learned more about Mrs Stevens and her family and felt duty bound to talk briefly about himself and his friendship with Brian. They had just finished when they heard voices coming towards the kitchen and Georgina called out, 'You're too late. It's all done but nice timing.'

They all returned to the lounge and played a couple of rubbers of bridge that Kit hadn't played since his days at university. Stella switched on the TV and said, 'I like to keep up with what is going on in the rest of the world. I kid myself that the BBC and the other lot are not too biased, unlike the papers which tend to hype up the news whatever it happens to be.' The evening was drawing to a close when Brian remembered he should have got in touch with base and asked if he could use the phone.

'You know where it is. Take your time.'

A brief call to the duty customs officer and he was told that the only news that concerned him was that the trial of the villains who had stolen the boat was now fixed for three days' time. It seemed that a previous trial had fallen through. The duty officer went on, 'I just have to get hold of Mr Tynan. He's not answering his phone. If you know where he is tell him to report at Ramsgate Court in three days' time at 10.00 to go through the proceedings with our lawyers. The trial starts after lunch.'

'Cheerio.' Brian ended the conversation and he and Kit said goodnight to Stella and Georgina and thanked them for a lovely evening.

On their way back to the boat where they intended to spend the night Brian told Kit about the message from the police. The next day was busy, making sure they knew what they needed to say and comparing notes. Kit phoned the Haven, explained about the trial and asked if he could stay there for a couple of days. 'No trouble,' was the reply. 'If you ring me when the trial is over I'll come and pick you up,' said Bert Matthews.

The trial lasted two days and almost from the start it seemed as though the culprits would get off or receive only a minor sentence. Kit was called as a witness and could scarcely recognise the two prisoners. They were well dressed, clean shaven and Kit was only asked two questions. He could state with some conviction why he was in Ramsgate and merely happened to be on hand to witness the accident at Ramsgate station. No he had not seen anyone attack Mr Chalmers although he had gone to his assistance. It was his own prosecuting council who gave Kit a worse time in trying to save the day and ensure that all the facts were revealed.

'Mr Tynan. Can you identify the two men in the dock as the two men who stole the motor launch and who were subsequently at Pegwell Bay.' The lawyer's voice was almost pleading.

'Yes Sir. Those are the two men who were rescued.'

'Do you know that they stole the boat?'

'I saw them at Ramsgate harbour and the next time they were being rescued by helicopter.'

'But you were some distance away. How can you be sure?'

'Yes. I saw them through binoculars and definitely recognised them.'

Then the defence lawyer got to work again. 'What if I told you that these poor men had permission to borrow the boat and were in fear for their lives when shots were fired at them.'

'I cannot comment on that statement.'

Kit was dismissed and felt that he had been asked the wrong questions. The police sergeant, sitting next to him, assured him that it was not his fault and that the police often had difficulty in bringing to justice suspects who had a devious lawyer. The boat owner was questioned at length but the two men stuck to their story. They had definitely been given permission to borrow the boat with a view to buying it from a friend. They knew nothing about the guns and had been intending to take it to Sandwich for the winter where they would meet the owner. They had certainly restrained someone they had found on board and intended to hand him over to the police when they reached Sandwich. The deciding point in the argument came when the so-called friend was produced. He corroborated their story but pointed out that they had mistakenly got the wrong boat. His boat was called Swordfish whereas the one they had taken was Spearfish. He even intimated that he was cross because he had been obliged to go and collect his own boat the next day. This was later corroborated by the harbour master.

The judge realised he had been hoodwinked by this latest twist. He could only fine the two men and make them pay for the loss of the dinghy. He also gave them 50 hours of community service, spread over the next five weeks. The police tried to insist that the men were guilty of aggravated assault on the boat owner and on Brian Chalmers. The men accepted that they had locked the owner in the toilet but completely denied the attack on the customs officer. They said they were very sorry for their genuine mistake and the trial was over.

Kit was upset at the way the case had gone and complained to the police. They had experienced it all before and intended to keep close tabs on the men especially now that they had to complete the community service. Although they never said as much Kit realised that the police were hoping that the culprits would slip up during the next month or so.

That the villains had got off very lightly was accepted by the police as par for the course. George Simpson issued an internal memo, part of which said, 'It is my considered opinion that the recent spate of fires are not connected. I believe that the news media are responsible for exaggerating the damage caused and the time consumed by the emergency services.' He approached his colleagues in Essex and Suffolk and they all agreed to call it a day although the cases would remain on file.

Brian reminded Kit about the boating lessons and it was agreed that they should stay in Ramsgate for another day. This gave Kit an opportunity to ask Bert Matthews about the possibility of going up the Stour as far as possible.

'What I'd really like to do would be to go by boat round the Isle of Thanet. I think that would make a good story, stopping off and chatting to the farmers. I've come to the conclusion that Thanet is not an island any more so the Stour is the next best thing.'

Bert considered his reply carefully. 'Actually Thanet is still an island but only just. You could start at Sandwich and follow the Stour to just past Plucks Gutter, then you'd have to go on to the Wantsum, a very much narrower channel and it goes all the way to Reculver on the north side of the island. You'd need a small canoe to complete the course. However, by launch you can certainly get as far as Canterbury.'

Kit listened intently as Bert explained, 'I'm not certain about getting through Canterbury but I'm pretty sure it can be done. We'll take one of my launches and I'll come with you.'

'That's marvellous. Thanks.' Kit said goodbye and caught the bus back down to the harbour to join Brian.

Kit didn't enquire too closely about where Brian had slept although he was fairly certain he hadn't been by himself. They returned to Whitstable and after a cup of coffee Kit said cheerio and set off for the Haven in his own car.

Part 2
Escape to Freedom

Prologue

In 1940 Holland was quickly overwhelmed with the surprise attack by the Nazi invaders, the indiscriminate bombing of her cities and the rapid advance by the German army. Although the fighting was over in a few days the stubborn resistance of the much smaller Dutch army was used by Germany to impose severe restrictions on the conquered population.

In peacetime the country produced plenty of food but with the occupation came privations. They continued to produce the food but most of it went to feed the enemy while the Dutch people were forced to exist on starvation rations.

By the winter of 1943 the fate of the population was becoming desperate. Even small towns and villages in the country fared little better. The stocks of food spirited away when the Germans first arrived in 1940 had now been used up or discovered by the Gestapo and removed. The Germans resented the resistance by the Dutch and even more so the fact that many from the homeland and even more from the Dutch possessions overseas, now occupied by Japanese forces, had somehow joined the Allies and were now employed in activities against the invaders.

In the winter of 1944 the situation had become much worse and people began to die of hunger, malnutrition and disease. Only in the really isolated places such as the West Frisian Islands or the farms on the north-west coast did the people manage to survive.

Into this region in 1943 came a detachment of German ack-ack batteries as a deterrent against the constant stream of Allied bombers on their way to Germany and among them was Hans Engels. He had seen service in Denmark, Germany and much earlier in France. Now, having been wounded in Russia he was among a few soldiers who were the vanguard of a convalescence unit though many more were to follow.

HOLLAND AND THE NORTH SEA

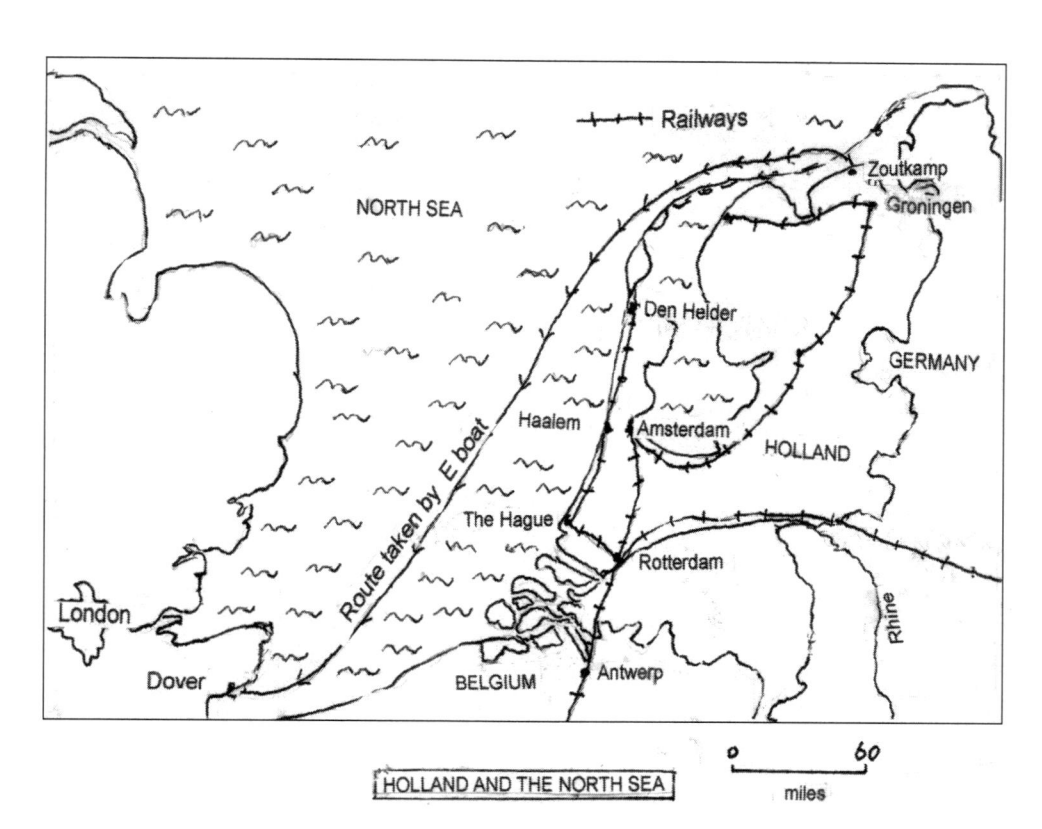

German E boat at speed

Chapter 10   A Chance Re-Union

In the north east corner of Holland is the provincial town of Groningen. It is on the River Reitdiep, on a slightly raised strip of land while all around the land is below sea level. It is 20 miles from the North Sea and only 25 miles from the German frontier. Gerda Blom waited outside the train station for her uncle and although there were several groups of people they spoke in hushed tones, not wishing to be overheard by nearby groups. Gerda waited alone, sitting on her suitcase.

A lorry arrived with a trailer and a man got down from the driving seat and came over to her, extended his hand in welcome and called out, 'You must be Gerda. I'm your uncle Wilhelm. You've grown a bit since you were last here.'

She got up and went towards him and he seemed to envelope her with his massive frame as he kissed her. Gerda was 15 and had been sent to stay with her aunt and uncle when the bombing of Amsterdam had been at its worst. Here, everything seemed unreal as she got into the lorry and they set off for the farm, some 20 miles away, near the village of Zoutkamp.

For her the destruction of Rotterdam had been left behind. The massed air raids on Amsterdam would remain with her for a long time but for the moment she was safe. That had been in May, 1940. She had settled into the daily routine of farm life and loved every minute of it, that is apart from the wind that blew across the low lying fields. Now, in October, 1943, a young woman of 18, she received admiring glances whenever she went into the village. She did most things on the farm and somehow in this backwater they managed to survive much better than the remainder of the country. About twice a year she visited her parents back in Amsterdam. Each time she managed to take them small amounts of dairy produce and eggs, carefully hidden about her person but larger amounts of food like potatoes and other root crops and joints of meat had to transported differently.

She travelled to Amsterdam by train but got off at the station before. It was closer to where she lived and although checks were made they were not as thorough as at the main stations. So she was able to smuggle in a ham joint, a joint of pork as well as root crops. These were carried in cardboard boxes that could be discarded should it become necessary. After each visit Gerda was relieved to get back to the farm. Travel in war time Holland was a hazardous undertaking.

At the farm the daily chores helped to ease the pain of being away from home and there were other distractions. A group of German soldiers moved into the area and commandeered one of the large barns for their personal use and told her uncle they also needed a large field in which to erect tents and temporary huts for about 150 men.

In the course of her work she often passed close to the barn. One of the soldiers called out. 'Good morning.' She had returned his greeting and continued on her way. During the next few days she puzzled over this casual meeting. The same soldier greeted her again and Gerda thought the face looked familiar and came to the conclusion that he might be Hans ... what was his name ... Engels. Now she remembered. He had been one of the German students who had camped on her uncle's farm before the war. She just happened to be spending her holiday there with her parents. He came to buy eggs, cheese and butter. 'That must have been in 1938. What a difference a few years make. Now they just take whatever they want,' she mused. She also recalled that in that holiday they had become quite good friends, had exchanged addresses and had actually corresponded for some time.

The farm, not far from Groningen, became a rehabilitation area for soldiers returning from the eastern front in Russia. It wasn't much of rest though for they were formed into platoons and did daily patrols along the coast to be on the lookout for possible invasion by the Allies. Even so it was a welcome respite from the bitter fighting in Russia and the food was considerably better than the stuff they usually had.

A week passed before she saw him again and this time she asked him his name. 'Yes. I'm Hans Engels and I'm very pleased to see you again. I thought it must be you, especially being on the same farm.'

The friendship formed some five years earlier gradually revived over the next few weeks and Gerda came to realise that not all Germans were as ruthless as the thugs who had destroyed her country. In hastily snatched moments together they gradually exchanged notes of what had happened to each other. In spite of the present circumstances a bond of friendship grew between them until one day Hans told her he was going back to Russia but would like to come and visit her after the war.

She instinctively went closer to him while he responded, and kissed her goodbye. He turned to go and never saw the truck that hit him. He was thrown a few yards and landed up by the barn door, gashed his head on a stone and dislocated his left shoulder.

This resulted in his posting being postponed and sent to hospital in Groningen where he recovered. Gerda was allowed to visit Hans. His dislocated shoulder was quickly put back while the gash to his head needed more attention. A week later he was allowed to return to the barn and saw Gerda two days later.

He was put on light duties and only had to go out on patrol every other day. On alternate days he was in the barn helping to prepare meals so Gerda was able to see him as she went about her work. If the officer was aware of this he said nothing. Hans discussed with her his fears and the way the war was going in Russia and tentatively at first and then quite openly said how shocked he was at the treatment of the Dutch people.

Gerda managed to see Hans almost every day. Then came a change in the weather. The sea breeze had dropped. The sun shone really warm and heralded a very hot day. She put on a light summer dress though she still wore her farm boots. She was determined to tackle Hans about his real feelings regarding the war.

While she and Hans had to be discreet about their meetings, the soldiers turned a blind eye while she was unaware of the remarks they made behind her back. Gerda went to the barn mid-morning when she knew they were having a break. The patrol had been out since 5.00 am and were glad to be dismissed. Hans walked over to where Gerda was sitting, grooming her dog.

'These patrols are a waste of time,' was his opening remark. 'We never see anyone trying to come ashore or leaving for that matter.'

'Good morning,' Gerda greeted Hans. 'How well do you know the navy boys down at the landing?'

'Oh, quite well. As a matter of fact one of them comes from my home town. Why do you ask?'

'I wonder if he could arrange for you to go out in his boat for a short trip and maybe I could come too.'

Hans got down next to her and his hand crept round her waist. It felt comforting and even when he gradually moved it upwards and touched her breast she did not object.

There was a sudden movement to their right as the men had finished their break and were about to go on patrol again. Hans and Gerda quickly got to their feet. He rejoined the patrol and she went back to the farmhouse.

Chapter 11 A Bold Plan

During his convalescence and on the days when he was not out on patrol Hans became a frequent visitor to the crew of the E Boat based at the small landing. It was a couple of miles to the coast but it was easy walking and the weather remained fine. The sailor, Karl Moyen, who came from his hometown, got quite pally although they not met previously. When the Lieutenant was away Hans managed to go out on short patrols and became accepted by other members of the crew. These patrols usually lasted no more than three or four hours, their main job was to look out for anyone trying to leave the country or enter it illegally. Their secondary task was to clear mines left there by the Royal Navy in hit and run tactics. On other days, longer patrols took them to hit and run raids in the Channel.

During their snatched moments together Hans mentioned his growing unease about Germany's invasion of Holland and the dreadful time he had experienced in Russia. Gerda commiserated with him but there was little time for them to be together although she sometimes got the feeling that he was not the only German who was fed up with the war.

Since their previous meeting Gerda had deliberately avoided meeting Hans. Now she made up her mind and just happened to be near the barn when they returned from their patrol. 'Hello Boys,' she greeted them. 'Nice weather for a walk,' and then sat down near the barn.

Soon, Hans came over to join her and said he was pleased to see her and wondered why he hadn't seen her for a few days. 'I've been thinking,' she replied. And then in a whisper, 'I haven't thought it through but if you really don't like the army you could desert. They would hunt you down and you'd be shot. But if we managed to borrow one of the E Boats we could escape to England. I speak quite good English and if I remember yours is not bad either.'

'It's a nice thought but we'd never get away with it.'

'If we don't try soon you'll be well enough to be sent back to the fighting. Go and ask your friend if we may both go for a little trip next time they go out. I'll bring him some eggs and butter as a bribe. Over the next few days and weeks if necessary I'll gather together a few supplies for the voyage. I'll be away for the next few days visiting my parents in Amsterdam. I'll see you when I get back.' With that remark, Gerda disappeared into the farmhouse.

At the back of her mind was the idea that if they managed to go out in the boat several times they might be able to observe how the crew managed such a powerful vessel.

She did in fact go to see her parents and took as many eggs and as much butter and cheese as she could smuggle about her person. She also took two packages of similar produce, one for her parents and one as a bribe for the guard. The guard was glad of the eggs, cheese and pork so let her through in the hope that there would be more on another trip

Her parents were overjoyed to see her and more than pleased with the gifts. She persuaded them to have a meal and hide the remainder. While they ate she told them of her plans to get to England though for the moment she left Hans out of the picture. She knew that her father had secretly taken some of his diamonds out of his safe at work. Some she thought would be hidden at home while others would be secure at his place of work while still more would be with friends.

She broached the next part of her plan with care. 'Would you like me to take some of your diamonds to England? They would be well hidden until I got there. I would of course have to tell the authorities or I could take them to the Dutch Embassy in London.'

It all sounded so plausible that she almost believed it herself. It wasn't until much later that she appreciated the enormity of the task she had undertaken. 'What do you think, Father? Have you any ideas? I could certainly do with your help. I should have no difficulty in getting away in a boat and once out in the Channel the British navy will pick me up and escort me to England. They come quite close to us at the coast to sow mines.'

To her surprise neither mother nor father said 'No' immediately. Then her father spoke. 'I've been considering such a move for some time, that is how I could get some diamonds to our embassy but never thought about this idea. Tomorrow, I want you to come with me to the city and meet the other dealers. Let me explain. When the bombing started we each deposited in the main vault a quarter of all our stock. You realise this is like currency and it wasn't long before the Germans demanded access to the diamonds. They obviously used it to purchase war weapons from so called neutral countries. Another quarter of our stock was put in each of the dealer's own private vault. A third quarter is at our homes and the remainder, mainly uncut diamonds could be anywhere. We each, individually know but we decided that if no one else knew they could not divulge the secret even under torture.'

'So you managed to save quite a bit'

'Well, yes, although from time to time they do make demands and we need to let them have some. They appreciate that if we release too much at once they would soon lose their value.'

'So what do you think of my plan?' asked Gerda.

'Come upstairs to my study and we'll talk while your mother has a little nap. I think there is some merit in it but I want you to meet Jon Klinder and get his opinion. If he thinks the idea is sound he will persuade the others. If not I will ask you to take mine into safe keeping. I am aware that you may be caught by the Germans and that you may not even reach England but you go with my blessing. I will not tell your mother so she will know nothing of our plans.'

'If you reach England get in touch with the Dutch Embassy and insist on speaking to Karl Lemmer who's an old friend. Some diamonds will provide you with funds to keep you going while the remainder the Dutch Embassy may use as they wish. They will give you a receipt for the diamonds. They will keep a copy and gradually dispose of the diamonds to help pay for our military forces. At last I shall be doing something to help the war effort.'

The following day, feeling like conspirators they walked to his place of work and she settled down in his office while he made a few phone calls. Jon Klinder arrived shortly after and made a great fuss of Gerda whom she vaguely remembered as a sort of uncle when she was younger. Her father did most of the talking while Jon listened. At the end he got up and was beaming all over his face. 'That's the best bit of news I've heard in years. Anything's worth a try in these dreadful times but this has the makings of success. I'll go and see a few of the others. If they are not interested I will definitely ask you to take a few of mine.'

On the way home scarcely a word passed between Gerda and her father, both mulling over in their heads the tremendous task that lay ahead and the possible consequences if it all went horribly wrong. She was a bit surprised that he carried a parcel under his arm. They were stopped twice. 'What's in the parcel,' the patrol wanted to know.

'Just a few bits of clothing that need washing. I've been meaning to get it done for ages. My daughter is staying with us and she has promised to do it for me.'

'Open it,' came the curt command.

'Certainly,' but it really is only old dusters, a pullover and a change of clothes.'

'OK get along.'

'Thank you,' replied her father, deferentially to the German.

'I thought you had the diamonds with you,' whispered Gerda.

'I did and I do. You need to keep a head on your shoulders when dealing with the Germans. The uncut stones are in a concealed compartment in my best hat and I can tell you it is mighty heavy. I shall be glad to take it off. The other diamonds are about my person – all told worth well in access of twenty million guilders and I have a secret collection at home. Also I haven't worn clogs in years and it's surprising how comfortable they are. These are rather special as they each have a small hollow section where I've secreted more stones.'

'I must say you were pretty calm. Maybe you should come to England with me.'

'I'd love to but I can't leave your mother and she would never leave home and her friends.'

'We'll say no more on the subject. I will try to let you know if I'm safe and if I am so will be the diamonds.'

The two conspirators continued on their way home and as a celebration had a meal of roast potatoes, roast pork followed by egg custard.

Chapter 12 — A Bagful of Trouble

After dinner her father went to his study and returned carrying four small leather bags of diamonds, each tied at the top with a leather thong. 'These are not all our worldly goods but they do represent a king's ransom. I'm keeping a few back. These days we may have to buy ourselves a bit more freedom though we have to be careful. Once they've got the diamonds we'll probably end up in a concentration camp or worse. Hide them carefully on the boat. By the way you haven't told us who is going with you.'

'It's a young lad who helps occasionally on the farm. He knows all about boats. I will provide the food for the journey and also help with the boat. He doesn't know about the diamonds. It's not that I don't trust him but the fewer people who know about them the better.' Gerda had wondered when this question might come up and was pleased that she had handled it so well though sorry that she had to lie to her father.

Early the following morning, she said farewell to her parents and caught the first of three trains back to the farm. The journey went well and at the end she waited for the bus to take her the final three miles to the farm. The driver said it had broken down and that it would take at least three hours to repair so Gerda decided to walk with a few other passengers. They walked a mile and her companions turned off the road to their home leaving Gerda to continue on her own.

Plodding along by herself she became conscious of a vehicle coming up behind her and stood to one side to allow it to pass. It was a German staff car and stopped a short distance in front of her and Lieutenant Simmen called out from the passenger seat, 'Can I give you a lift, Miss?'

She vaguely recognised him as one of the officers from the base on her uncle's farm. 'Yes. Thank you. I'm going to my farm but the bus has broken down.' He opened the rear door for her and in a matter of ten minutes she was back at the farm. She thanked the officer and hurried in to greet her aunt and uncle.

After dinner Gerda went to her room and really for the first time began to think about her hair-brained scheme of escaping, to borrow an E Boat, elude the German navy and air force, dodge the mines, make contact with the British navy and arrive safely in England. It had all seemed so plausible when she had first thought of the idea. Now she had the small matter of getting Hans to finally agree and of course the equally small matter of actually stealing a boat.

One other thing worried her. Hans was still recovering from his accident but it could not be long before he would be sent back to the fighting and away from this backwater of the war. The opportunity to see him came the next day as she passed by the barn where several soldiers were billeted. He was outside peeling a huge mound of potatoes and preparing other vegetables for their main meal.

'Have you got any meat to go with those?' she asked.

'No, but we're used to not having any.'

'I'll go and persuade my uncle to let you have a couple of hares. They make lovely stew or hot pot.'

She returned with two hares. 'I'm afraid you'll have to skin them or I could do one for you.'

He thanked her and then said, 'When can I see you? I'm on patrol tomorrow.'

'I'll come back about seven tonight.' The time dragged but just before the agreed time she made her way to the barn with a couple of eggs.'

Hans at once told her the good news. 'My sailor friend has made arrangements for me to go out with them the day after tomorrow and I've asked him if you may come as well. He thinks it will all right as the Lieutenant is away again. Meet here about 10.00 in the morning and we'll just walk down to the quay. It's only about two kilometres.'

Gerda didn't sleep very well that night. She kept turning over in her mind all the things she had to do and then worried about all the things that might go wrong. Finally she did sleep only to wake up in a cold sweat to find the Lieutenant grinning down at her. 'So you thought you'd escape from me.' The dream had been so vivid but she did the sensible thing. She lay down and allowed her heart to stop racing.

It was 5.30 but she decided to get up. There was still work to be done on the farm and a few more supplies for the voyage to be hidden away for when they set out for England. She hoped the voyage would take no more than seven hours so she decided to take just one meal of bread, butter and cheese. She added a few apples and a jar of soup. She did not want to alarm any of the crew so decided to take only a change of underclothes but felt that a raincoat would not be considered out of the ordinary for a short trip.

She considered that the authorities in England would provide her with everything she needed. After all, she would be bringing them an E Boat. In the quietness of her bedroom she opened one of the bags her father had given her. There were at least a dozen, fairly large and beautifully cut diamonds. She had never really taken much interest in diamonds but these sparkled and seemed to come alive in the candlelight. Then in one of the three smaller bags she found almost a hundred smaller stones, all beautifully cut. She had no idea of their value but her father had said they were worth a small fortune.

Finally, she opened the third and fourth bags in which were quite large diamonds, some uncut, though even to her untrained eye she appreciated that they too must be very valuable and as she held them in her hands she knew exactly where she would hide some of them. Some of the real diamonds could be hidden about her person but the large uncut ones would have a special hiding place. Other diamonds would be hidden in the bra she was wearing. They might be a bit uncomfortable but if well padded surely no one would notice she had an extra three centimetres on her bust.

Among other things that Gerda had brought with her to the farm as a child in 1940 was an almost useless toy, the model of a child's windmill water pump and well. She had treasured it as a child of five. The pond was about five inches in diameter and the well which kept the water about two and a half inches deep. The pump at one side had a handle and when the pond had water in it the water came out of a spout. What had originally attracted her to it was the colour in the pond, iridescent shades of green and blue and little painted fish. That and an old pack of cards and a few crayon pencils had been all she had been able to bring with her.

Now, remembering her father's inventiveness in hiding the diamonds in his hat and more in the hollowed out pair of clogs had given her an idea. Carefully she prised open the bottom of the pond. Beneath there was about five centimetres of space into which she slipped all the uncut stones and so that they didn't rattle she melted two large candles over them and replaced the coloured bottom. When the paper didn't quite meet she sealed it with more melted candle wax and then filled it up with water and tried the pump. It worked and she actually said out loud, 'What a clever girl you are.' She did much the same with the well, hiding the stones beneath the original paper. The final hiding place would have to be found on the boat. The whole toy was only five inches high so, placed on its side it would easily fit inside her small suit case which she had finally decided she could smuggle on to the boat under her raincoat. The final hiding place would be in a money belt next to her skin and which she had yet to make.

Chapter 13   Boating with the Enemy

After breakfast she wandered over to the barn, met Hans and together they walked casually towards the jetty. Han's friend, Karl from his home town, was waiting for them at the base and ushered them aboard and asked them to go below. Two other members of the crew were on board and introductions were quickly made. Soon they felt the throb of the engines as the motors were started and then the gentle movement as the boat pulled away from its moorings.

Once out in the open water the visitors were allowed to come up and enjoy the thrill as they ploughed through the water at 40 knots. Suddenly Karl asked, 'I suppose you'd like to take a turn at the wheel. Just do everything gently. If you turn the wheel too quickly at this speed we could be in serious trouble. Your course is 005 degrees. Look at the compass.' It wasn't much of a lesson in handing the powerful E-boat but they were able to go out twice more and on each occasion they learned a little bit more about handling the boat.

Hans couldn't believe his luck. His new friend was actually showing him how to steer the boat, alter her speed and so on. This was probably the very boat he intended to borrow for their trip across the channel. The only problem was for his naval friends because with a bit of luck he would not be bringing it back. He knew full well the sort of trouble they would have if the officer got a hint of their secret boat trips. Hans eased off the throttles slightly and then gently moved them forward again to bring the speed back to the original setting. He made a mental note that the slower the speed had an effect on the steering.

Hans asked. 'Will this course take us to England?'

'Oh, no. You need at least 15 degrees to port. Probably a course of 265 would take you to Dover but you don't want to go there. Too many mines for a start! No, we are just doing our normal patrol along the coast to make sure that no one is trying to leave unofficially. It's a bit of a secret really but we sometimes do go across the channel in company with other E boats and play havoc with English coastal shipping that are carrying coal and other freight from port to port. I suppose our bombing has disrupted their rail network so this is their only way to move heavy goods around.'

Once again Hans eased off the throttles pulling all three together and turned the wheel and then ran parallel to the coast some three kilometres from the shore.

The sea was getting a little bit choppy with waves breaking over the boat and Hans was advised to put on some oilskins. Then Gerda was asked if she'd like to join Hans, on deck, borrowed some oilskins and tentatively took the wheel for a few minutes.

After an hour they had to turn back and resume their patrol in the opposite direction. Soon the two guests were taken on a brief tour of the vessel with their guide pointing out where the torpedoes were kept and where the torpedo tubes were at the front. They were even told that some boats had tubes at the stern to fire at enemy shipping enabling them to make a quick getaway. They were surprised how much space there was below decks although much of it was taken up with storage cells for fuel. They saw where some of the crew slept if time permitted. 'Try this bunk out for size miss,' suggested one of the crew. 'I could come up and stop you from falling out,' he continued with a knowing leer on his face. 'In your dreams lad,' replied Gerda and shoved him away as she got down from the bunk. He didn't seem particularly put out by the rebuff but for the remainder of the voyage Gerda kept well away from him.

Up on deck once more Karl waxed lyrical about the speed of the boat, how many ships they had already sunk, how much fuel they carried and how far it could go. He also showed them how many guns they had on board and was sorry he couldn't demonstrate their capability.

'Where do you eat? You never showed us.' Gerda wanted to know.

'We have a small galley. We are not usually out for more than five or six hours at a time but we could cook anything we wanted. If you're really interested we'll start at the stern again and gradually work our way along to the sharp end. Hang on to the rail until you get your sea legs. Can't have you falling over the side. You're not supposed to be here so I couldn't put that in the log. We have to make a note of what we do on each trip.'

Hans and Gerda both agreed they would like a more thorough look over the boat. Karl called to Axel, 'Take over will you while I show our guests over the boat.'

All three moved towards the stern. As they stood looking over the stern at the wake the new helmsman suddenly slowed the engines and then speeded up again with the consequence that Gerda nearly fell overboard.

Axel called out, 'Sorry. A bit of driftwood got in the way.'

Somehow she didn't believe him and had the distinct impression that he was paying her back for refusing his earlier crude advances but said nothing. Instead she concentrated on all that Karl said as they gradually moved forward. Any little bit of information might come in useful during their planned voyage.

'All the brass work has been painted over.' Gerda thought she should show some interest.

'It's kept dull so that it doesn't reflect sunlight. That's the short answer,' replied Karl. 'So here we are amidships. We have to be a very low profile but there's plenty of boat below so we just step down a little bit and we have a number of cabins and storage compartments for stuff of all description and of course the ammunition. If we go out sowing mines they are carried on deck as well as torps.'

Back in the wheelhouse Gerda made a face at Axel. He said nothing. During this patrol they had met no other shipping, received two radio messages and sent out two. All too soon their sea trip came to an end as they had to return to base, the patrol's work for the day completed. Gerda took the trouble to thank each of the crew and over the next few days made a point of putting by some eggs and butter for Hans to take to them. By mid afternoon they were back on shore. As she and Hans walked back to the farm they spoke only briefly about the possible trip to England. 'Do you really think you know enough about the boat to sail her away,' asked Gerda. 'And can the two of us really get away with it. I don't suppose it's any good trying to recruit a member of the crew to come with us.'

'I am a little concerned. I expect you are, too,' replied Hans. 'We'd be foolish if we weren't. I don't think it would be wise to tell anyone else, let alone invite them along. We'll get to England or die in the attempt. Are you having second thoughts?'

'No. None at all. Everything is planned – not every detail. On the day, whenever that is we shall take the boat and once under way we shall just play the cards as they fall. That is what I think.' Gerda stopped talking and looked directly at Hans. 'Is it OK with you?'

'Sure thing,' he replied. They parted as they reached the barn.

Her aunt was worried at her long absence but she explained that she had been talking to the sailors at the jetty and had lost track of time. A week passed slowly during which they managed another two trips on the boat and then it was Friday with the Lieutenant off on leave though only for 48 hours. When Gerda heard this news she decided that this was an opportunity not to be missed. If they didn't attempt to go now the chance might not come again. Hans would soon have to go back to the war and one other factor finally made the choice easier. Her aunt and uncle had been invited to a friend's 60th birthday party in Gronigen. After they had left on the Friday night she would pack everything for the voyage, clothes in her suitcase that also contained the toy pump, all the food and of course the diamonds that were in several different places. One was in a money belt next to her skin while a second bag was concealed in her suitcase and another small bag which she hoped to conceal on the boat once they were under way. More diamonds lay comfortably in her bra. The final lot was stitched into the lining of her raincoat.

As soon as her aunt and uncle had left for Groningen and all was ready she walked casually out towards the barn and managed to see Hans and explained that everything was ready as far as she was concerned. Much to her surprised he agreed at once and said very early on Saturday morning would be the best time before anyone was about. They quickly made their plans and agreed to meet up at 3.0 o'clock. She didn't sleep very well that night so she was up quite early on Saturday. Like fugitives, that is precisely what they were, she and Hans walked slowly towards the jetty. Gerda looked distinctly plump as she had put on extra clothes and a big coat under which she carried her small suitcase, suspended from her neck with a long piece of webbing. Hans looked remarkably smart in his uniform although he also took his greatcoat and a rifle.

'What on earth made you bring that,' she asked.

'Well, you never know when it might come in handy.'

They met nobody and stepped quickly on to the E boat. Hans took the precaution of dropping a length of rope over the side of the second E boat near the stern in the hope that when and if they were followed the rope might foul the propellers. He cast off fore and aft while Gerda disappeared below to hide her diamonds and other things and to stow her overcoat and was quite relieved to put her suitcase on one of the bunks.

Now seemed to be as good a time as any to look for a suitable hiding place for the diamonds. Those in the windmill toy would remain in her suitcase as well as the package behind the false back of the case.. Those tucked away in a home-made belt next to her skin were only slightly uncomfortable. They served to remind her of the importance of their escape. Another hiding place, obvious though not necessarily for someone quickly searching in her case was in a flat package tied up with her laundered handkerchiefs. She had earlier debated with herself if she should keep all the stones together. On balance she decided to keep them in several separate bags, hoping that if one was discovered the others might not be found. Here in the cabin she found a hiding place behind a bulkhead, easy to retrieve when the time came and not too noticeable.

She was surprised that so much of the boat was made of wood. She remembered that Karl had told them that earlier boats were made completely of wood. Only the more recent ones had metal hulls and a small amount of armour plating in vital parts. They mainly relied on their speed to get away.

The outgoing tide carried them slowly away from the quay and out towards the sea. The boat seemed to know its own way as she headed away from the shore. Now would come their first test – to start the engines. Hans had seen it done many times but could he do it now! He switched on the fuel, primed the engines and pressed the starter.

Chapter 14   No Turning Back

The engines burst into life with a thunderous roar that threatened to wake the whole neighbourhood. Hans immediately closed the throttles and gently eased them forward again as the boat got under way. He checked everything as quickly as he could and allowed the speed to creep up to 10 knots. A glance towards the shore assured him that no one had stirred.

It all seemed too good to be true – and it was. One of the crew members, Axel, the very one who had upset Gerda by his suggestive remarks last week had decided to sleep on board after a night of beer drinking. The motion of the boat finally woke him and still the worse for wear, he staggered up to the deck. By this time Gerda had finished hiding the diamonds and she too was on deck just a minute or so before he arrived. The first person he saw was Gerda and he lunged drunkenly towards her. As she moved away he turned and saw Hans at the helm and recognised him.

'Where are we? And what are you doing here?'

'We're heading for England. You have two choices. You can either come with us or we'll drop you over the side and you can swim ashore.'

He lunged at Hans who easily sidestepped and grappled with the sailor. Axel lashed out and caught Hans on the side of his head opening up the gash again and momentarily stunning him. While he struggled to get up the sailor was all over him. Gerda picked up the first thing that came to hand, the rifle that Hans had propped up against the side of the cabin. She picked it up, reversed it and swung it with all her might at the sailor.

With Hans still pinned to the deck Axel's head was the first thing she aimed for. The pent up feeling of anger and the frustration that their escape might be in jeopardy gave her added strength as she aimed the blow. She heard his skull crack as the rifle butt came down. The second blow struck him on his shoulders. Axel stopped fighting and lay still, silently moaning while Hans was able to ease himself from under the inert body. Gerda was very concerned for Hans and went below to look for a first aid box. Once back on deck she cleaned the wound, applied a dressing and persuaded him to sit down. She remembered the heading that would take them to England and turned the boat until it was heading in the right direction, according to the compass. She then set the engine speed to 20 knots and lashed the steering wheel to keep on course.

She then went below again and made some coffee. When these events were later related she surprised herself that she had remained so calm. The unfortunate Axel remained where he had fallen and his moans had ceased. With hot coffee to warm them and heading towards England everything appeared to be as they had planned. Hans recovered slowly and although his head still ached he was well enough to steer the boat while Gerda stood on top of the cabin and kept a look out for mines.

She asked Hans to take a look at the German sailor and then, for a moment, was sorry when Hans said that he was dead. Together they heaved him over the side and watched his body disappeared as the boat surged forward. They said nothing.

The early morning mist had promised a fine day but it had given way to a misty fine drizzle of rain. They reduced speed but visibility was down to about 200 metres. She was getting very wet and was glad she had found the oilskins. With a sailor's cap on her head she certainly looked the part.

While Hans took the wheel Gerda tried to make head and tail of the charts. They were more complicated than she had realised, nothing like the maps used on the land. She made out various wrecks noted on the chart as well as the details of the depth of the ocean. She had supposed it to be level but there were various rises and falls. Then there appeared to be a series of signs where the Germans had anchored mines so that they floated just below the surface while others could be visible on top of the waves.

She voiced her concern and Hans agreed. 'From now on we'll wear life jackets and if we hit a mine the first thing to do is to inflate the jacket by pulling the little toggle. If we are about to sink and we are still alive at least we'll float.'

Gerda was surprised at this casual response but assumed that as a soldier it might be the only way to survive what he had already been through. She went down below and found two life jackets and Hans showed her how they must be put on to remain secure.

She went below again to make more coffee and looked into three cabins and came across the one where the unfortunate Axel had spent the night. There were four empty beer bottles on the deck and two more full ones secured on a little shelf above the bunk. The coffee went down well and she took one up for

Hans and offered to take the wheel while he went below. He declined the offer to relieve him, saying he felt better in the open and that they really needed two pairs of eyes to look out for mines.

He glanced at his watch and could scarcely believe that so much had happened in just two hours from leaving the jetty. It was now only 5.0 o'clock and they had no idea where they were. The sea remained calm with only the swell causing the boat to rise and fall as it continued on its way. He had heard about Atlantic rollers where the waves dropped 40 feet or more. Here in the English Channel it seemed almost as bad. It was really nothing like that but unpleasant all the same. He wondered if he sailed west for say half an hour and then a little bit north and then east if this zigzag pattern be any better.

He never got the opportunity to try it. Out of the gloom, more or less on a parallel course, a ship appeared. It was flying a white flag with a small Union Jack in one corner. The British navy had arrived and it fired a shot over the E boat. Not knowing quite what to do Gerda and Hans did nothing while the ships continued on the same heading. Another shot, this time much closer and a loud hailer spoke in German, 'Heave to or we sink you.'

Hans quickly waved a white handkerchief and hoped that would do the trick. Gerda quickly went below and returned with a sheet from the officer's bunk. She gave one end to Hans while she held the other. Hans cut the engines and they both watched the other boat.

Chapter 15   The Royal Navy Arrives

The British ship also stopped and appeared not exactly menacing but its sheer size compared to the smaller E boat was threatening enough without its large guns that were now trained on to the German boat.

A pinnace was lowered but did not travel in a straight line towards the E boat. It steered way over to the starboard allowing a clear field of fire for the guns at the slightest sign of action on the part of the enemy.

As the pinnace got closer Gerda called out in English, 'Good morning. Can you give us a tow? 'We want to get to England.'

The next ten minutes seemed like an hour but at last the navy men climbed aboard and the questions began. 'Who are you?. Why do you want to get to England? Where is the rest of the crew? What nationality are you? We are going to search this boat with you still on board just in case there are any booby-traps.'

Gerda replied as best she could. 'I'm Gerda Blom from Holland. This is Hans Engels. He is a German soldier who helped me steal the E boat. I need to get to the Dutch Embassy in London. There is so little food in Holland that many people are dying of starvation and the embassy needs to know this.'

Suddenly all her bravado evaporated and she burst into tears and sobbed while the bewildered navy man tried to comfort her as best he could to the amusement of his comrades. While this was going on the crew detailed to search the vessel looked in the most likely places where explosives might have been placed. Twenty minutes later they signalled the frigate to come alongside so that the refugees could step up on to the larger ship. The skeleton crew remained on board and the two ships set off for England.

Once on board the navy ship they expected more question but it seemed that the captain who had been told the gist of their story was happy to provide them with hot drinks and for them to relax until they reached England when he knew the real interrogation would begin. After an hour, while the ships changed course several times in order to sail within safe sea lanes, the frigate drew alongside the harbour wall at Dover so that Gerda and Hans under close escort could walk off the ship.

Once ashore she remembered her suitcase, large coat and other items. She asked if she could return to collect her belongings. The navy was courteous but said 'No.' They were taking no chances that she might trigger some device that would blow up the ship. A sailor was detailed to retrieve them and later handed over to her. A quick glance through her suitcase revealed that it had been searched, though not thoroughly, for her childhood windmill pump was still there and the false bottom on the case had not been touched. Gerda, anxious to retrieve the hidden package of diamond on the boat would have to try again.

Gerda and Hans were separated and still under escort. Captain Reynolds introduced himself and said he'd like to ask Gerda a few questions and then Introduced Lt. Rogers as his assistant. The questions were quite straightforward, name, address, reasons for entering England illegally and so. What was her relation to the German soldier?

'Well Sir,' Gerda explained, ' I lived in Amsterdam. When the Germans invaded I went to live with my aunt and uncle on their farm near Groningen. In 1938, I think, I was also there on holiday when a group of German students came to camp for a week or so. That's where I first met Hans Engels and we became pen friends. He was sent to the farm in 1943 as a sort of rest from the fighting in Russia and was billeted in one of the barns. We met again purely by chance. We talked briefly about the possibility of escaping and he became friendly with the E boat crews. And they took us out in the boats a few times.'

'On Saturday, today, we sneaked away and were out to sea when one of the sailors who had slept on board woke up and came on deck. He started fighting and pinned Hans to the deck so I hit him with a rifle butt. He died soon after so we tipped him overboard. '

'That really is my story except that I do need to see the Dutch Embassy in London. Also there is so little food in Holland that people are dying of hunger. The Dutch government here need to know this.'

'I'm afraid that is not possible but give me the message and will pass it on.'

Gerda was tempted but stuck to the script she had been given by her father. 'Sorry, Sir. I can't do that. It's from my father and he insisted that I spoke directly to someone from the embassy. Mr Karl Lemmer is the man I should contact.'

'Leave it with me. I'll see if I can arrange something. There will be further questions. Usually, foreign nationals who turn up on our shores are interned. You are one of our allies so will be treated differently. You will certainly meet Dutch officials and they will surely want to help you. I must congratulate you on your command of English.'

Her interrogator got up. 'Please remain here and turned to go. At the door he turned round, smiled and said in fluent German, 'Sprechen sie Deutsch.'

Gerda was not put out and replied in French, 'I also speak German and English but I don't let everyone know that. It shall be our little secret.' She smiled as she said this and Captain Reynolds came back into the room.

'Sorry about that I wasn't really trying to trick you. I admire you. I'll go and sort out this embassy business for you. Goodbye. Let me introduce Lt. Page.'

The Wren, Lt Page, who had remained just behind the captain said, 'If you would like something to eat will you follow me to our mess. You can have whatever you want, that is if they've got it. I'm your escort for the time being. Welcome to England.'

Meanwhile, Hans was being questioned along similar lines though perhaps not in such a friendly manner. He was able to tell them his regiment and his unit and they were able to check that he had been in Russia. In fact he was surprised how much his interrogator seemed to know about his unit's activities in Russia including the three retreats they had been forced to make.

As to his escape his answers tallied closely to those that Gerda had given. There were a few discrepancies, enough for them to be authentic. Hans accepted that he would now be a prisoner of war. The officer had one bit of advice. 'You will be questioned very carefully by your fellow POWs. That gash on your head needs to be looked at properly but it could be used to your advantage. It adds a certain credibility that you were abducted by a British raiding party. You need to have a good story as to why you suddenly turn up out of the blue.'

Hans thanked the navy man and he was then taken to the mess, still under escort, to join Gerda. They were ordered to speak in English as their escort did not speak Dutch or German. Gerda asked about his wounded head while he could see that she had recovered her composure. They seemed surprised that so much food was available. It was long past the usual lunch break but the meal was more than adequate – plenty of potatoes, pickle, red cabbage and three slices of lamb. This was followed by stewed apples and custard, followed by tea or coffee. Both enjoyed their first taste of English food while Hans joked, 'I wish I'd come over to you sooner.'

After lunch they were taken to a rest room where there was a billiards table, table tennis, books and newspapers. They seemed to have been there for hours, still with their escorts. The navy man had offered Hans a cigarette and then given him a whole packet and some matches while Gerda's female escort chatted about clothes, hair and make-up saying that there was a small shop, a NAAFI, that opened at 6.0 o'clock where she could purchase a few personal items. Then the original interrogation officer came into the room with two very distinguished looking men in grey suits.

Chapter 16 — Helping Hands

Two very smartly dressed men arrived from the Dutch Embassy and Gerda was summoned to meet them. They looked Dutch but she could not be sure so she spoke to them first in German and then in Dutch. One of them laughed and said, 'You are right to be cautious but we don't play tricks with our own citizens. I know your father well. You may ask any questions about him. I know, for example, that he has a birth mark on his left hand near the wrist.'

'Absolutely correct. Good afternoon, Mr Lemmer,' replied Gerda. 'Can you also tell me what the children sometimes called you when you were learning English. Please write it down on a piece of paper and hand it to me.'

'That's a long time ago. I had almost forgotten. This is the word. Quite nice really.' He handed her a piece of paper on which he had written a single word LEMON and said, 'I believe you have a message for me.'

'Not quite a message. More of a gift for which I shall require a receipt. You must sign a copy of the receipt and after the war I will present my receipt to you and you will give me back my package or what is left of it.'

She reached into her suitcase and brought out a bag of diamonds, opened it and poured out the stones on to the table. Both officials were staggered as they gazed at the stones that sparkled under the lights. They were speechless. Not so Captain Reynolds. He merely exploded with 'Hells Bells.'

Gerda explained, 'I understand that these represent a small fortune. They are from my father and are to be used to buy whatever is necessary to help the war effort.'

Mr Lemmer replied, 'I'm no expert but I reckon they are worth at least four million guilders. We are running out of money so they will certainly come in handy. I'm joking of course. I'm very glad the British navy didn't sink you. I must say you took a big risk bringing them here.'

Captain Reynolds added, 'I'll have to put my chaps on a charge for not finding them when they searched the boat.'

Gerda had combined the diamonds hidden in her bra with those from the handkerchief package. 'They wouldn't have found them,' she replied. 'With an impish grin on her face she brought out another bag and handed it over. They wouldn't have found these either.'

Mr Lemmer quickly untied the bag and once more literally poured out its contents on to the polished table. About a hundred diamonds cascaded on to the table as Gerda explained that these were not quite so large and so not as valuable but still quite useful.

Mr Lemmer was the first to recover from this second gift. 'I hope your father is aware of the consequences if the Germans ever found out about these.'

'I was also worried at first but he had a reasonable explanation. He will tell them that if they hadn't made such a devastating bombing attack on Amsterdam the diamonds would still be there. As it happens they were bombed and now lie at the bottom of the harbour.

Gerda turned to Captain Reynolds. 'Perhaps you'd like to look in my suitcase.' The navy man took out a few clothes, her little windmill and a book. He checked to see if there was a false bottom but could find no evidence. Just about to give up he realised that the back side of the small case near the hinges seemed a little too thick. 'Do you want me to take away the lining,' and receiving a nod from Gerda he carefully pulled aside the lining to reveal a flat package that he put on the table.

Gerda split the package and emptied the contents on to the table. Another collection of stones joined the growing fortune. Gerda said, 'I know it's not the right season, but Happy Christmas.'

'You haven't got any more little treasures tucked away have you,' asked Reynolds.

'Only this one,' she replied, holding up her right hand. On the third finger was a platinum ring with a single large oblong emerald surrounded by eleven small diamonds. It's really for my 21st birthday but father gave it to me a few years in advance. He actually made it on my last visit to Amsterdam when he asked me to look after these for you.'

The meeting was drawing to a close. Mr Lemmer asked, 'I wonder Captain, if I ought to have an escort on my way back to London.'

'If you think it necessary Sir, I shall arrange it. Miss Blom and the diamonds are now your problem. Her release from us has just been approved.'

Mr Lemmer said, 'If Miss Blom is willing I'm sure we can find work for her at the embassy. With her knowledge of English and German there would be plenty for her to do and she'd be paid, not in diamonds but in English pound notes. This will all take a few days to arrange but in the meantime we will provide her with any clothes that she needs and she can stay at the embassy until other arrangements can be made.'

Gerda spoke. 'I have two questions. The first is, What happens to Hans Engels?

The navy man explained, 'The German soldier is now a prisoner of war and will be handed over to the military, probably tomorrow. At this stage of the war I doubt if he'll be sent to Canada with other POWs so he will remain in England. He will be allowed to write to his parents and to you miss on alternate months. That is if you still wish to correspond with him.'

Gerda felt she should explain. 'He is really a pen friend who I met before the war . By pure chance we met again at the farm. However, if it hadn't been for him I would not have got away and you wouldn't have your diamonds. So I will write to him. Can I ask that he be treated well.'

'I shall certainly pass on that request.'

'My second question is about the E boat. What happens to it?'

Captain Reynolds explained that it would form part of the growing collection of enemy ships that had been captured. 'We might even use it against the German navy,' he joked.

In the excitement of the arrival of the navy, actually being in England, the questions and everything else that had happened, she only now remembered the final bag of diamonds that she had hidden behind the bulkhead of the third cabin on the E boat.

With everything now going smoothly, with the promise of work at the embassy she somehow was reluctant to tell them about the other diamonds.

This Document is a Receipt for an Enemy Warship, namely, a German E boat, Presented to the Royal Navy by Miss Gerda Blom, a Dutch National. With a Friend she, Borrowed the Vessel, that was Moored near her Uncle's Farm at Groningen in Holland. The Vessel was Escorted into Dover Harbour by HMS Wellfit. The E boat is on Loan to the Royal Navy for the Duration of the War. At the End of Hostilities it is to be returned to Miss Blom as a Prize of War, on production of the Receipt.

Signed W. Reynolds. Captain. RN

Receipt for the E Boat

Instead she said, 'What really happens to the boat. Years ago, according to tradition, it would have belonged to me.'

Captain Reynolds smiled, 'I'm afraid those days have long gone. The boat will be put to good use , I assure you.'

Mr Lemmer felt he should support his countrywoman. 'Surely, Captain Reynolds, prize money is still available and shared among the crew who capture an enemy vessel. If it hadn't been for this young lady you wouldn't have an enemy ship to use. Is there not some long forgotten rule that would eventually give her ownership. If it survived the war it would be hers.' He winked at the navy man and said, 'May I leave it with you. A little research into the rules of prize money should not take too long. You may then hand me the document and I would keep it for Miss Blom.'

'I'm sure you are right Sir, leave it with me. If there is such a rule I might just go and get me an enemy boat for myself.'

'Is it possible to see Hans before we leave. I ought to thank him and explain that I will write. I need to give him my address. I assume he can send a letter to me at the Dutch Embassy.'

'Yes. That will be fine. Tell him to put TS after your name. It stands for Temporary Staff, not very grand but we've had a lot of new people since the war.'

Hans and Gerda met briefly. She told him not to worry as captain Reynolds had promised he would see that he was well treated. She also explained about writing to her. He thanked her and said that with such an adventure they had both shared it was one they would remember for a long time. She kissed him lightly on the cheek and they parted.

Then began the long journey back to London. For Gerda it was another new beginning and she looked forward to this one, feeling somehow safe and secure even though the bombs continued to fall.

Chapter 17　　　　　Safe at Last

The journey back to London passed fairly quickly. There was little traffic on the road and tonight the German Air Force decided to stay at home. Mr Lemmer explained that he would introduce Gerda to some members of the embassy staff tomorrow and that, at least for tonight, she would have a bed and her own room. Most of the journey passed in silence, Gerda wrapped up in her own thoughts and Mr Lemmer anxious about getting the diamonds safely inside the embassy.

Nearing the capital he pointed out a few notable buildings although by now it was getting dark. Gerda was surprised that so many buildings were in ruins and also by the number of people who were feeling their way around the city during the blackout. 'They are theatre goers returning home after visiting a theatre,' explained Mr Lemmer.

Gerda ventured one question. 'Is there any way I can let my father know that I have arrived and that you now have the diamonds?'

'There are certainly ways but they all take time. I will put the wheels in motion tomorrow and, who knows, you may even receive a reply. Briefly we send out a radio message, in code of course. Someone in the Dutch resistance receives it and eventually it will reach your father. At this stage I'll not tell you how this is done. It's not that I don't trust you but the fewer people who know what goes on the better.'

The car drew up outside the embassy and taking various pieces of luggage and brief cases Gerda and Mr Lemmer and his aide went inside.

From that point on Gerda's life was almost planned for her. At times she thought that the finger of fate had already written her destiny but she was happy enough. She met new friends at the embassy and eventually more in the outside world and was grateful for the comparative safety of London.

Work for her inside the embassy was, initially, nothing more demanding than opening the mail and putting it into pigeon holes to be taken to designated departments by special messengers. Once she had proved her worth she was moved to other sections, gaining experience all the time and being surprised by the number of enquiries that came from people living in the Dutch overseas possessions.

Some of the letters had taken months to arrive and had been written by relatives anxious to trace their families in Holland. The embassy tried to find out about the families though sometimes the areas where they had lived in Holland had been destroyed by the bombing. When they came to reply to the letters the senders often had been forced to leave because of the Japanese or had just vanished.

Though heartbreaking such stories were, Gerda appreciated how important this work was in the hope that after the war families might be reunited. Her meticulous work in cross referencing and indexing these details was much appreciated by her immediate department head.

She made many friends at the embassy, many of them like her had just happened to arrive on the scene. One in particular, was especially helpful in finding a small room in the house where she lived. It was only five minutes' walk from the embassy but it ensured a degree of freedom away from work, freedom which over the coming months she cherished.

The enforced separation from Hans Engels was suddenly brought home to her when his first letter as a prisoner of war arrived. She immediately felt guilty as she had temporarily forgotten about him. His letter was informative though not really personal in the way she might have expected. He was in a camp in the north of England. He was well treated, the food was good and after a month he had joined a working party to help out on a small farm. There were five POWs and an armed guard. They were taken to the farm each day in a lorry, had a mid-day meal there and were driven back to the camp in late afternoon to have an evening meal. He did not mention their escape but said he would write again soon. He hoped she was well and sent his best regards. As a letter, she thought it might have been dictated for him.

Even so she was pleased to know he was well and replied immediately. Over the next several months his letters continued, each one telling her about his work on the farm, about his fellow Germans he worked with and that they accepted his story of how he had been captured. Gradually his letters seemed to change, to be more personal and slightly inventive, especially the relationship that they had enjoyed It was done quite subtly so that Gerda, who realised what was happening, actually began to believe a more than casual friendship had existed until his latest letter arrived.

My Dearest Gerda, Work at the farm continues. Now it is spring and the winter wheat that was sown last year is coming up nicely. Everything is beginning to grow again and the first of the lambs have been born. When the farmer knew that I had been on a farm he has allowed me to help with the animals and even got permission for me to help with the lambing. I was allowed to stay overnight and sleep out in the field. It was very cold but we managed to snuggle down among the bales of hay. I'm mentioning all this because I have been giving some thought to our future life together when the war is over. I remember you once telling me you would like to be a farmer's wife, not a city dweller. I remember the fine time we had together on your uncle's farm. I'm sure you also remember how we sneaked away and your aunt was so cross because we were late back and you hadn't told her we would be away.

Yours ever, Hans xx

Gerda read the letter several times. Was he trying to tell her something in code or was he imagining the things he had implied. In the end she sought a meeting with Mr Lemmer. She wanted to know how she should reply once she had explained that as far as she was concerned there were never any romantic incidents. Should she just reply and hope that he understood the situation or would it be possible to go and see him. Perhaps, writing as he had he really did have a special message for her.

'Leave it with me,' said Mr Lemmer. ' I have no idea how this can be managed but I know a man who may be able to help.'

'Thank you, Sir. I'm sorry I had to trouble you.'

'That's no trouble. I only hope we can arrange something. How are you getting on? I hear good reports of your work here. Your father is well and sends his love. Anything else, don't hesitate to ask me.'

'Goodbye, Sir and thank you.'

Two weeks went by. Gerda had not replied to the letter and then Mr Lemmer sent for her.

'Good morning Gerda. This gentleman, Col. Leiden, is going to escort you to a farm in the north of England. You may need to stay somewhere overnight so take some night things. We have arranged a meeting with Hans Engels on the farm where he works. Col Leiden will be with you all the time though he will be very discreet so that you and Hans will be virtually on your own and able to speak freely. I can give no advice so do what you feel is right for you both. He will go back to the camp as usual so no one need be any wiser unless he chooses to tell them. You will be leaving tomorrow morning at 7.30.'

The meeting was over and Gerda smiled her thanks and went back to work. The following morning she sat in the rear seat of the embassy car next to Col. Leiden. He made polite conversation and she responded speaking in their own language. After a while he took out a whole sheaf of papers from his brief case and got on with his own work. Most of the time was taken up by Gerda looking out at the ever changing scenery as the car sped northwards.

After four hours they stopped for lunch at an army barracks and soon afterwards they were on their way once more. Another hour and they stopped outside a farmhouse. 'Please remain here, Miss Blom. I'll just make sure everything is ready,' explained the colonel. He returned a few moments later and opened the door. 'Please come with me.'

They were met by an English soldier at the front door who ushered them into a drawing room. Hans Engels sat at a desk and got up as they entered. It took Gerda a few seconds to recognise him though Hans knew her at once. He grinned at her and held out his hand in welcome. 'They told me I had a visitor but I never expected it to be you. I'm so glad to see you.'

'Hello Hans. You're looking well. This is a really special surprise arranged by the Dutch Embassy. We may have a few moments together and you should not mention this meeting to anyone else. If there is anything that you need, let me know and I will try to get it for you.'

Hans was completely surprised by the visit and scarcely knew what to say. He explained that he was well, that his headaches had completely gone and that he was being treated well as were all the inmates of the camp but most of all he loved working on the farm.

This was her opening to remind him of his comments in his most recent letter. 'Please explain what you meant by us becoming farmers . While I also like farming I have never considered us having a farm together.'

Hans smiled. 'I'm so sorry. That would be wonderful. One gets to dream all sorts of things. Perhaps I didn't explain myself clearly. My letters to you always cover the same ground. I wanted the people who read them, you know they are censored, I wanted them to know that I am a little bit different. I'm sorry if my letters upset you. I'll be more careful in future.'

'I thought you were trying to tell me something in code but just couldn't work out what it might be.'

By now they were both smiling. They began to talk about life on her uncle's farm, the good times and those not so good and for a moment they forgot the two other people in the room. Then it was time for the return journey. The soldier and the embassy man went out first. Gerda kissed Hans briefly and said 'I owe you a letter, but I will not mention this meeting. Goodbye.'

On the way back to London Gerda reflected that she had been pleased to see Hans and was glad the meeting had gone well. In fact she now realised there had been no hidden agenda in his letters, perhaps just wishful thinking for someone far from home.

Two months later came the D day landings and almost a year's hard slog across Europe to victory and VE Day. A few weeks later came the surrender of the Japanese and VJ Day and the war was over.

Chapter 18　　　　　　　　Married

With everything in turmoil after peace had been achieved, especially in Europe, there were millions of people in the wrong place, most of them anxious to return home to their families. For many of them their homes no longer existed. It was also an opportunity for some to assume new identities and to seek out new destinies

Since the meeting between Hans and Gerda in 1944 the content of their letters to each other had gradually changed. From remembering times as pen friends prior to the war to relief as successful co-conspirators who had stolen an E boat from the German navy and made their escape to England. The letters had changed significantly, thankfulness that they had survived and there now seemed to be real friendship and on occasions even a hint of affection and love.

In July 1945 Hans was about to be repatriated and wrote to Gerda asking her what he should do. Her reply surprised him. Among other things she had written, *'I think you should propose to me properly. I would then have to consider what your prospects are likely to be and if you could keep me in the manner to which I have become accustomed. (joke), I might even say, Yes. I have told Mr Lemmer how we feel about each other and he has suggested a very feasible plan. I assume this letter will be censored so I really need to see you to discuss possible plans with you.*

I could travel to you if you are able to get out of camp or if you are still working at the farm I could meet you there if you tell me where it is. Remember, I was driven there in 1944 in an official embassy car. Please let me know as soon as possible.' She had signed the letter, *Love from Gerda*.

The reply from Hans arrived almost by return post.

My Dear Gerda,

How wonderful to receive your most intriguing letter. I had to read it three times, especially the bit at the beginning about getting married. I'm sure you know this is what I have wanted for so long. I never dreamed it could happen so that is why I never mentioned it. You really are the most kind, generous and lovely young woman a poor German soldier could hope to marry.

It seems that I am still a prisoner of war until I am handed over to the Red Cross or I am returned to my own country. Some of my comrades have already gone but I have volunteered to continue at the farm for a little bit longer. That is probably the best place for us to meet. I go there each day, sometimes on a Sunday from 8.0 in the morning to 4.0 in the afternoon. The address is:-

Gerda's reply to this emphasised how carefully they should proceed from now on. She intimated that from conversations she had with Mr Lemmer, he was convinced that he would be able to get Hans transferred into his care on the understanding that he would be returned to his country of origin. Having checked train times and local bus connections nearer the farm she sent Hans a time and a date when she could meet him. She warned him that trains were still a bit unreliable so she might be delayed.

A week later she set off quite early. The train was on time although she had to change at York to catch the local train to Malham. From there she had a choice of a local bus or a taxi. As the bus had just departed and the next one was not for another two hours she elected to go by taxi and half an hour later arrived in style at Hillside Farm. She asked if she might call the taxi driver in a couple of hours. He agreed but suggested he call at 4.0 o'clock. This would give her time to catch the local train to York which in turn would enable her to catch the London train.

When they met Hans and Gerda were, initially, awkward between each other, not knowing whether to shake hands or kiss. In the end they did both and then laughed. Mrs Browne had greeted them, showed them into the sitting room, brought them tea and home-made buns and left them together.

They were still laughing when Hans asked, 'Would you really like to be my wife? Technically, I'm still an enemy soldier. One thing I am sure about is that I love you. I would be so proud to be your husband. I know there will be enormous difficulties when we get back home but where is home. Tell me that.'

'That's the strange thing,' explained Gerda. Mr Meller suggests that you change your name into its equivalent in Dutch. As you have no passport you will be issued with a new one. It seems that many people have lost theirs and he says one more passport will not make any difference. If you agree to this he assured me that not too many questions will be asked about your sudden appearance.'

'All this needs to be finalised but Mr Lemmer is convinced it is the easiest way if we want to be together. If you go back to Germany there is nothing there for you. You told me in one of your letters that your mother had died and that your father had died earlier in the previous war.'

This meeting with Hans, which in some ways, Gerda had been dreading, seemed to be going forward in a most friendly way. She was still not convinced that she should marry him, wondering if she had been caught up in the romance of the circumstances. She was also not quite sure about Hans and his real feelings for her. She had kept from him all knowledge about the diamonds she carried into Britain but she did just wonder whether somehow he had guessed and that they were the reason that he wanted to marry her. Not a very sound basis to begin married life. She thought.

'I hope you don't mind me making these arrangements for you or that I'm trying to run your life. Of course if you have a girlfriend at home you'd like to find I will not stand in your way.' As soon as she had uttered the words she regretted them. Having virtually asked Hans to marry her she was now giving him the opportunity to back out. Surely just a few minutes ago he had declared his love for her. She felt awful.

'I'm sorry Hans. I just needed to make absolutely sure. I do love you. I shall be honoured to be your wife. Now I must leave you to return to London. I'm going to ask Mr Lemmer to give me away and if he can trace Captain Reynolds, who actually captured us maybe he might like to be your best man. I will write to you here in future.'

They held each other for a moment kissed passionately for the very first time and Gerda was finally reassured. Mrs Browne called to say the taxi was waiting and Gerda thanked her and asked if it would be in order to send letters to the farm.

'Of course. No trouble at all. Hans is a nice young man and a good worker. We shall miss him when he goes.'

Back in London Gerda set wheels in motion about her forthcoming marriage, surprised by her ready acceptance of the subterfuge. Although she understood only a small part of the workings at the embassy she was astonished that it condoned and actively encouraged such activities. She couldn't believe hers was an isolated case permitted just because she had brought over the diamonds.

The wedding was set for four weeks ahead to be held in a small church not far from the Dutch Embassy. The new passport for Hans had been produced. It stated, among other things that he had escaped in 1940 and managed to get into France and reached the British soldiers at Dunkirk. Here he had actually helped in the evacuation and subsequently travelled to England in one of the small boats.

During her time in England Gerda had, occasionally managed to get a message to her father in Holland. Now she wrote a fairly lengthy letter, attempting to explain all that had happened to her. She told him about her engagement and that as they couldn't get a proper engagement ring she hoped he wouldn't mind if she used the ring he had given to her for her 21st birthday. She drafted several different versions of the letter until she was satisfied with the news about getting married before coming home. She also explained that travel to Europe was extremely limited for civilians so it might be some time before they could actually come home.

Gerda and Hans were married by the padre attached to the embassy. Mr Meller gave away the bride and Captain Reynolds was happy to be the best man. He had asked one of his crew to make a model of HMS Wellfit, the ship he had captained when he first met the happy couple. Mr Meller presented them with a framed document about the German E boat that stated that the boat had been donated by Miss Gerda Blom for use by the Royal Navy for the duration of the war and should be returned at the end of hostilities.

The married couple were thrilled with these unexpected gifts and Gerda asked, 'When do I get the boat?'

'I've no idea,' replied the Captain, suddenly realising she was quite serious. 'As a matter of fact I think it was bought by a chap in Folkestone. I will make enquiries and be in touch.'

Three months went by before they were able to get a flight in an American Liberator, being used to ferry military personnel from place to place. It was a bit uncomfortable but it was better than waiting for a ship. They went first to Amsterdam where Hans was made very welcome by her family. Gerda was at last able to hand over the uncut diamonds hidden in her toy windmill. Her father asked her to accompany him to work so that he could explain their sudden re-appearance. The members listened with amazement to the story of the chequered history of their diamonds. They were worth considerably more now and the committee decided to award Gerda the difference in cash and to present her with a written commendation that also included Hans. With this money she bought a farm near her uncle's and over the next few years they worked and they farmed and they diversified and they prospered. They also had two children, a boy and a girl.

It was several years, not until 1960 that Gerda thought about the diamonds still hidden in the E boat, wherever that may be. She decided to tell Hans the whole story and then told her father. He immediately set about trying to find the whereabouts of the E boat with little hope of ever finding what had happened to her.

He wrote to his old friend in the Dutch Parliament, Joseph Tilberg who was the minister for Naval Affairs. It seems that boats are important commodities and records of their ownership are kept centrally. By liaison with the British Naval Attache, with so little to go on, over the next several months they were able to find out that during the war it had been used on several occasions against the German navy and for raids on the Dutch coast. After the war it had been sold at auction to a certain Albert Thomas, an ex-navy man who lived at Folkestone. All the warlike equipment had been removed and although she kept her drab grey colour he had made a meagre living by showing people over her and taking them for trips during the summer months.

It was expensive to maintain so eventually he put it up for sale. The chap who bought it, Jonathan Greenaway, could not afford the harbour dues at Folkestone or even those at Ramsgate so he moved it up the River Stour as far as Plucks Gutter. Here there was free mooring and he hoped to gradually sell off any valuable pieces of equipment. He had managed to remove all three engines and many of the mahogany doors and other pieces of furniture. He was in the process of hiring a firm to cut the boat up and sell it for scrap when he died.

'So where is the boat now?' Gerda wanted to know.

'It's still up the river at Plucks Gutter,' replied the captain. 'I'm sure if you got in touch with the British authorities they would come to some arrangement. It's probably termed a wreck now so that would involve another authority. Would you like me to find out?' Captain Reynolds was trying to make amends, 'I'm no longer in the navy but I keep in touch with old friends. I'll sort something out and let you know what I find.'

'That would be the thing to do. I'd like to see it once more. After all we owe it a last goodbye as it brought us to England.' Gerda at first thought there was little hope of finding the boat but with this knowledge she was determined to make the effort. She decided that they would all have a short holiday in England.

Part 3
The Curious Affair at Pucks Gutter

Prologue

Plucks Gutter is on the map if you look carefully. A large map of the Isle of Thanet that also includes a few miles to west that takes in Sandwich is required.

It is an inconspicuous dot on the map with one pub, a caravan park and a few houses. It is also on the River Stour which at this point is only 22 feet wide though when the tide is in or when the rains come it fills up to about 32 feet.

The pub's clientele are mostly farmers who work the local farms but it is also a convenient distance from Margate and Ramsgate for motorists to travel during summer evenings for a quite acceptable meal. Many fishermen also spend hours along the river bank waiting for a bite and then wander along to the pub for a pint and to talk about the ones that got away.

In the history of the Isle of Thanet nothing has ever been recorded of significance that happened at Plucks Gutter until ...

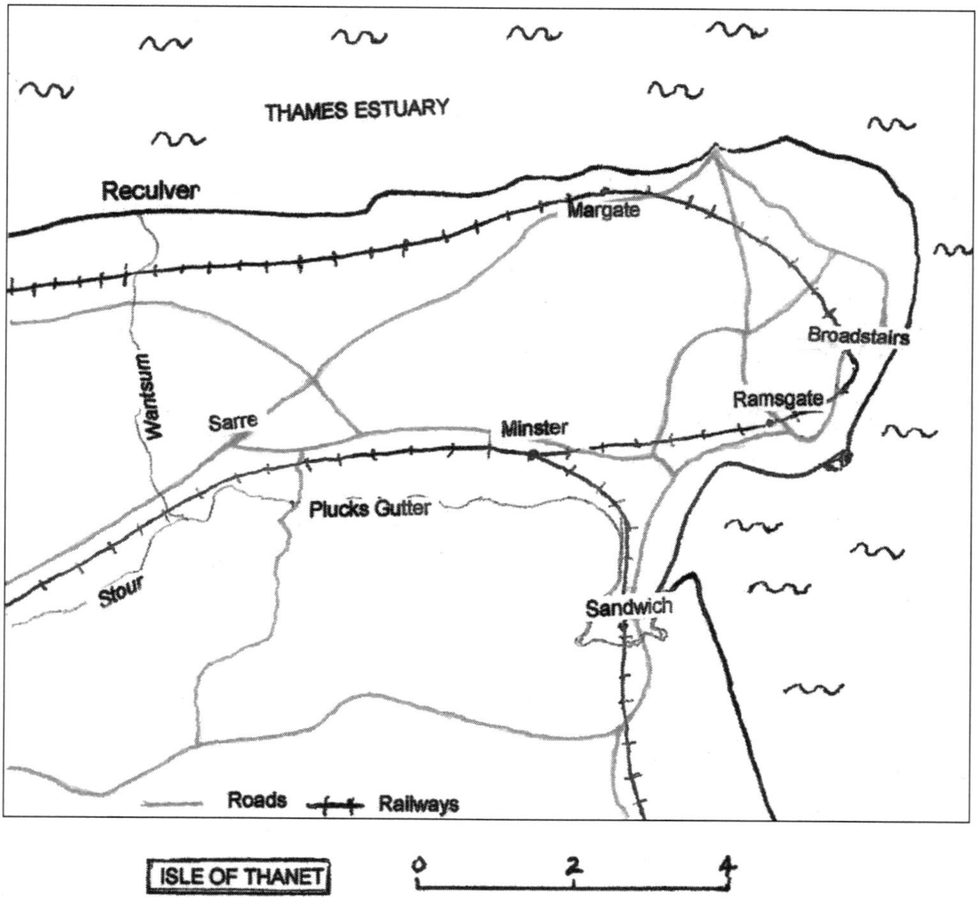
THAMES ESTUARY
Reculver
Margate
Broadstairs
Ramsgate
Wantsum
Sarre
Minster
Plucks Gutter
Stour
Sandwich
Roads
Railways
ISLE OF THANET
0
2
4
miles

Chapter 19 Thanet is an Island

'There's no way you can take the launch from Sandwich to Reculver. You'd get so far and then have to take to the dinghy. Better still a collapsible canoe might come in handy. Even then I doubt if the stream north of Sarre is wide enough.' That was the opinion of Bert Matthews when Kit broached the subject yet again. Kit realised that the older man's local knowledge made sense. He still thought it might be nice to make the effort. If he couldn't reach Reculver on the North Kent coast he could return to the place where the river divided and head for Canterbury.

'OK. I bow to your superior knowledge. Will you come with me as far as Plucks Gutter?'

'Sure,' replied Bert Matthews. If we start out from Ramsgate early we should be there by tea time. Beryl can pick me up in her car. I can't stay any longer as we have a lot of people the next day for their annual get-together.'

They 'borrowed' sufficient stores from Beryl's larder and stowed them on the Landrover ready for an early start. The remainder of the evening was given over to a few pints round the fire and checking the map and tide tables. Friday morning and the weather looked promising. Beryl drove them to Ramsgate harbour and then returned to The Haven to prepare for the people who were coming on Saturday. It was unusually late in the year for so many to descend on The Haven. However, with most of them opting for self catering, Beryl would manage with just two part time staff.

It was a matter of a few minutes to unload the stores and transfer them to the launch. A quick goodbye to her husband and Beryl was on her way up the long road out of Ramsgate. Matthews obtained clearance from the harbour master and received the latest weather report. The only open water they had to cover was from the harbour to the river mouth at Pegwell Bay. Once there, it would be merely a question of observing the rules of river navigation.

As they cleared the harbour wall and began to cross the bay Kit remembered the last time he was here. Then, watching from the shore, he had seen a similar launch run aground while being pursued by the Ramsgate lifeboat, the RAF and police. All was now peaceful and there was plenty of water beneath the boat as she held steady for the river.

Sandwich itself is a very small town that can become quite congested when travelling by road. Its narrow streets and overhanging houses almost present an obstacle course. Large numbers of visitors to this ancient port make matters worse. Today, on the river, the launch moved quickly through the town and was soon surrounded by fields.

'On either side the river lie

Long fields of barley and of rye.

Kit remembered these lines from *The Lady of Shalott*.

The barley in the fields had long since been cut and safely gathered in and one field had already been ploughed ready for the winter wheat. A mile and a half past Sandwich the river flowed quite close to the Roman fort of Rutupiae. From the river its ruins looked quite impressive and as the launch glided slowly on its way Kit remarked, 'You know, Pauline and I visited the castle a week or so back. It's quite large inside. The historians have done their stuff and show what it was like when the Roman legions were here. It was their major entry port to Britain.'

Not to be outdone by the history lesson, Bert replied, 'Did you know that during the First World War this whole area of Richborough was a secret port. Tons and tons of stores including all sorts of munitions left here for the troops in France. It is said that the Germans never discovered it.'

They stopped for lunch and a brew up at midday a mile or so south of Minster where the land all around was low lying and not very interesting. Bert couldn't resist telling Kit, 'You wouldn't have thought that when the Romans were here this river was four miles wide.'

'Maybe I should have come here 2000 years ago', replied Kit.

After lunch the thin, watery sun finally gave up the struggle and disappeared while a dull overcast sky turned the fields into drab colours. Threatening clouds from the west quickly overtook the boat and by 3.0 o'clock the first large spots of rain hit them. 'So much for an Indian Summer', said Matthews. 'The weather forecast this morning was completely wrong. Maybe it will be a summer shower designed to keep us on our toes.'

As they continued the rain became heavier. The cabin roof had been drawn over and the rain on the now enclosed cockpit was deafening while the windscreen wipers struggled to clear away the water. Walkers along the tow path had long since disappeared and the only boats they passed were either moored close in to the bank or had been completely taken out of the water and securely tied down on the river bank for the winter.

The downpour began to ease slightly and then the bridge over the river at Plucks Gutter came into view. Kit eased back on the throttles, allowing the boat to glide silently towards the landing stage until a quick burst in reverse and a slight touch on the wheel brought the launch close enough for Bert to step ashore and secure it fore and aft. They quickly put out fenders and then walked towards the steps and crossed the road to the pub. As they shook their oilskins in the porch the landlord opened the door and said, 'Come in gents and go and sit by the fire. What can I get you?'

'I think a couple of brandies would keep us going,' replied Kit.

The warmth from the fire and another brandy apiece worked wonders and soon Kit and Bert began to relax, just glad to be indoors. They sat by the fire and were content to remain silent. No other guests were in the pub and the landlord left them to their thoughts.

Plucks Gutter is some 15 miles from the river mouth at Pegwell Bay although only four and a half as the crow flies. The B2046 crosses the River Stour at that point. There is a pub, a small caravan site and not much else.

At this point the river is still tidal and when the tide is out it's not a pretty sight. Although only five feet of mud is exposed on each side of the river bank a small navigable channel remains in the middle. However, on a hot summer's day the exposed mud and decaying vegetation produces a stench that only goes with the next incoming tide. Some 200 yards west of the bridge the river splits into two, the Little Stour follows a south-westerly route while the Great Stour meanders its way to Canterbury and beyond. Half a mile from the bridge at Plucks Gutter the Great Stour also splits, one arm going north and becomes the River Wantsum. It almost loses its way and becomes very narrow until it enters the sea at Reculver on the north Kent coast. Because of its lack of water locals have been known to call it Want Some, that is, want some water.

However it wasn't always so narrow. Centuries earlier the Roman lighthouse at Reculver marked the wide channel that stretched down to their fort at Rutupiae. It was partly this remnant of history that fascinated Kit and the fact that he had decided to go up river as far as possible. There was also another reason and he wasn't sure when that idea first entered his head. It was possible that Pauline would be going home for the weekend and she might like to make a slight diversion and have a meal with him before continuing to her home.

As it happened Beryl arrived earlier than expected so after a quick exchange of greetings she and Bert said goodbye and returned home. Kit called Canterbury University and asked to be put through to the Language Department.

He asked to speak to Pauline Matthews. 'Just a moment, Sir. She has just left this office I'll see if I can catch her.'

Chapter 20 Rendezvous on the River

Kit couldn't believe his luck. He had anticipated a long wait, giving him time to think out how he should pose his question. Pauline came to the phone quickly so he had no time to think of persuasive points if her answer was No.

'Hello Pauline. Hope you don't mind me calling you at the university. I'm at Plucks Gutter and your mum and dad have just left. I wonder if you'd like to join me for a meal. I've looked at the map and it's only a small diversion off your normal route home.'

'Good afternoon Kit. Lovely to hear from you. You only just caught me. I'd love to have a meal with you. I know where it is and can be with you in about half an hour. I haven't got anything nice to wear.'

'You always look nice whatever you wear. I thought we'd have a meal on the launch but it's a bit chilly so we could have one in the pub. They have quite a nice menu. You can decide when you get here.'

'OK. See you soon.'

'Take care. I expect the roads are slippery after all the rain and mud washed down from the fields.'

'Don't worry. You forget, I'm a country girl at heart.'

Kit returned to the bar and asked the landlord if he could purchase a bottle of wine. 'Sure,' replied the man. It will not be very pleasant on your boat tonight. We do an excellent dinner here. Saturdays and Sundays are pretty busy but I don't expect we'll get many in tonight. In fact we've only got six people staying here at the moment – a family from Holland and a couple of Germans who are here for the fishing.' Kit thanked him. 'I'll wait till my fiancée arrives. She can decide.' Kit wondered later, why he had upgraded his relationship with Pauline.

The rain was easing off and in another five minutes it had stopped altogether and though now too late for the sun to make any impression it looked as though it might be a dry evening. He wandered over to the launch to check that he had enough in the freezer for a choice of meals. He returned to the pub and having reached the top of the steps from the towpath he looked out over the countryside. It looked drab and uninviting. He noticed for the first time that moored on the opposite bank almost level with his launch was a partly submerged grey launch. He guessed that in its prime it would have been a very fast naval vessel and it worried him that anyone could allow such neglect.

He mentioned it to the landlord when he entered the pub. 'To my knowledge that has been there for the past five years. It's a private landing stage on the other side. Pity really for I could have become rich on mooring fees.'

'How did it happen?'

'At one time everything was spick and span. It's quite roomy inside now that they have re-arranged part of it. It used to be a German E boat. After the war someone brought it over and it was eventually sold to a young couple. They kept it in Ramsgate harbour. Then an uncle who owns a few acres on the other side said they could moor it there for free. So each winter they brought it up here. The man was taken ill and died soon afterwards and his wife lost interest. One weekend some yobs from Sturry set fire to it and punched a hole in the hull. It's been like that ever since.'

'Could I go and have a look over it tomorrow?

'I wouldn't recommend it. It's full of mud and water and each time the tide comes in it helps to sink the boat a little bit further into the mud. One slip and you would have some difficulty getting out.'

The sound of a motorbike reached Kit's ears and he excused himself. 'I expect that will be Pauline. I'll see you later.'

Kit went outside to see Pauline arrive. She waved and drove round the back of the pub but soon re-appeared. She was just as he had seen her the first time when she had given him a lift from Margate station to her parents' home. 'See. I've brought the fine weather. It's stopped raining.' They kissed and went inside.

At the bar Pauline asked for a coffee and Kit said he'd like one so they moved over to the fire while it was being prepared. 'So you made it this far. How did you get on with dad?'

'Oh we get along fine. We always have. I had planned a nice little meal on the launch and you can still have that but it has got a little chilly so I'm wondering if you'd prefer to eat here in the restaurant. It's up to you.'

Pauline thought for a moment and then gave her answer. 'On balance I think I'd prefer to eat here. Let's see what they've got'

Kit returned with the menu. Pauline glanced quickly through it. 'I like all of them. You choose while I phone mum to tell her where I am and that I'll late.'

Kit chose lamb shanks in a rich sauce with potatoes, carrots, red cabbage and broccoli. At the bar Pauline seemed to be in conversation with the landlord. 'I don't think I'll drive back to Margate tonight if you have a small room for me.'

'And what about your fiancé?' Without batting an eyelid Pauline replied, 'He'll sleep on the boat.'

'Sorry Miss. We're full up. Our other guests, a Dutch family have a double and two singles and our other singles have been taken by two German gentlemen.' Just then, his wife who had just come into the bar explained, 'She can have the double at the front. It's not let until tomorrow night. We'll only charge you the single rate.'

'That is most kind of you. Thank you. I'll just phone my parents and tell them not to expect me.'

Pauline joined Kit near the fire. 'I'm staying here tonight so I can have another drink. What would you like?'

'I'll have a brandy, please,' said the astonished Kit.

They sat by the fire drinking while their meal was being prepared. 'So what sort of a day have you had?' Kit wanted to know.

'The usual Friday – trying to catch up on all the stuff we missed during the week. What about you?'

'Getting here with your father. My thanks to Brian Chalmers who gave me a few lessons on handling the launch and your father for letting me be skipper on his boat up the river.'

Their meal was ready so they made their way to the restaurant. The waiter appeared with Kit's bottle of wine that he had bought earlier and then the meal arrived. 'Lovely,' exclaimed Pauline. My favourite. You are a clever boy.'

The meal was eaten with scarcely a word passing between them but it wasn't an awkward silence. Once, when their eyes met, Pauline smiled and winked. 'I bet you can't tell what I'm thinking.'

Quick as a flash Kit responded. 'Please, not at the dinner table.' Between them they finished the bottle of wine. That, plus the food and the previous brandies was very comforting. 'I think we'd better have coffee. If you go over to the lounge I'll nip over to the launch and get the charts. I'll show you where I'd like to go and where we may have to go – that is if you would still like to come with me.

Chapter 21   River of Mud

Kit returned to the boat and because of the earlier squall decided to check the mooring ropes and ensure that the fenders were still in place. The tide had started to come in and as he looked across at the E boat he saw that the water was now lapping over the gunwales and into the cabin. The muddy banks were getting covered but the water in the river was like a sea of mud.

He got the charts, tucked them inside his shirt, leaving both hands free, and started to walk back to the pub. The sudden gust of wind hit him with such force that it almost knocked him over. And then came the rain, hitting him like stair rods. There was no shelter along the tow path so he struggled on and in no time was soaked to the skin. The path was now slippery and in trying to be careful and hurry out of the squall he slipped and fell over, grazing the side of his head on a stone bollard.

He lay still, almost grateful that there was no wind at ground level. Suddenly the storm had spent itself out as quickly as it had arrived. He carefully got up, appreciated that he appeared to have no broken bones although his head ached and it was bleeding. He was twenty yards from the pub and fifty from the boat so decided to head for the pub. Just as he was about to go up the steps the light on the tow path went out. The sudden plunge into darkness didn't help his staggering gait as he stumbled on. It was a bit of an effort getting up the steps but here all the lights were on. He pushed open the pub door and almost fell in as the door was opened by someone on the other side.

Kit had been gone a long time so Pauline put on her coat and started out to look for him when he almost fell on to her. 'I'm just coming to look for you.'

'Well, here I am.'

'Are you alright?'

'Not sure.'

She could see he was having some difficulty and helped him into the warmth of the pub. Kit slumped down onto the nearest seat while Pauline went to the bar and spoke to the landlord. 'I hope you can help me. My fiancé has fallen over. Could you give me a hand with him up to my room. I'm not letting him sleep on the boat tonight. Is that alright with you? Bill me for a double room.'

'Yes Miss. Don't worry. We'll get him sorted.'

Kit, still not really with it, managed to climb the stairs and sat down on a chair in the bedroom. 'Not there, my love,' said Pauline. 'Into the bath and get warmed up.

The landlord helped Kit into the bath and came out with his wet clothes. 'I'll get these dried off in the laundry room in a couple of hours. In the meantime he can borrow the bathrobe.'

'Thank you so much. One more thing. Could we have a couple more brandies. One is for me to get over the shock. The other one's for Kit to warm him up again.'

Pauline called out to Kit, 'Do you need any help in there?'

Kit replied, 'I can't find the soap.'

'Tough,' she answered. 'You're only there to get warm not to have a bath. Come out when you're ready and use the bathrobe. The landlord has gone to get you a brandy and your clothes will be returned soon.'

Kit stayed in the warm bath several minutes but finally got out, dried himself, put on the robe and returned to the bedroom.

'I'm sorry to give you this trouble, Pauline.'

'You're no trouble. Come here. Are you feeling a little easier now. She put her arms around him and kissed him full on the lips. I don't usually have naked men in my bedroom so behave yourself. As soon as your clothes come back I'll have a bath. In the meantime we'll have a look at the maps if you still feel up to it.'

Which, strange to relate is exactly what they did, checking the likely places where they might go, where they could stop for lunch and tea and how far beyond Canterbury they could travel. Kit had given up the idea of the north fork of the river. One glance at the chart had convinced him that they could not go more than a couple of miles. There was no room to turn round so they would have to reverse all the way back.

As the evening progressed, the hot bath and the brandy helped to ease any ill effects from his drenching and the fall. He appreciated that he would have a bruise on the side of his head tomorrow but the bleeding had stopped.

Almost two hours had elapsed when a maid knocked on the door and returned his clothes, washed, dried and ironed. 'Thank you,' said Pauline. 'Can you put it on my bill?'

'There's no charge, Madame,' replied the girl.

'Just a moment.' Pauline fumbled in her bag and gave the girl a couple of pounds.'

'Thank you,' and off she went.

'Now you can put your clothes on young man and I'm going to have my bath.'

Kit disappeared into the bathroom, put his clothes on, added keys and other bits and pieces to his pockets as well as his wallet. He returned the robe to its hook.

While Pauline was having her bath he glanced through the magazines in the room – a quite useful collection of local guides and a specially created folder containing local walks and places to visit in the neighbourhood. Pauline came into the room and joined Kit at the small table to look through the magazines.

'Pull back the curtains, Kit. Let's see what the weather is like.' The rain had stopped and the clouds moved quickly across the sky, allowing the moon to shine through occasionally, casting long shadows over the sodden ground.

After a while Pauline said, 'I don't know about you but I'm ready for some sleep.'

Kit reached out for his oilskins and said, 'OK. I'll see you in the morning and thank you.'

'And where do you think you are going?'

'To the boat.'

'You are not. You are staying here. I'm frightened of the shadows so I need you to look after me. Just lock the door and look the other way for a moment. No. Don't look in the wardrobe mirror. Just turn round and shut your eyes.'

Kit did as he was told. Pauline quickly took off the bathrobe and snuggled into bed. 'OK. You can look now. You may kiss me good night.' As Kit again did as he was told, she whispered, 'If you're very good you may come and sleep in my bed. It's not your birthday is it?'

Kit hastily removed his clothes and got into bed. 'Turn over,' she said, 'and I'll cuddle you. Goodnight.'

Chapter 22 Raised Voices

They heard doors banging as the other guests came up to their rooms and then all was quiet for a while until the locals started to go home. Everyone seemed to have a car and each had two or three goes before they managed to get the doors shut. Finally peace descended. It had been a long day but finally Kit and Pauline fell asleep without another word spoken between them

It was the muddle of voices that first roused Kit. He turned towards Pauline but she was already awake. He could feel her warm body next to his and reached out to touch her. As his hand caressed the contours of her slender form, she whispered, 'Listen and behave.'

The babble of sound increased until it was quite clear – voices speaking in a foreign tongue that Kit vaguely knew but couldn't understand. Pauline whispered, 'They're having a row next door, sometimes in German, sometimes in Dutch. Something about a treasure that belongs to one lot and the others are demanding a share.'

'How do you know?' Kit never knew what she did at the university.

'I study European languages at the university. There's one lot speaking in German. They seem to be the aggressive ones, while the others, a female and a man are obviously Dutch. They want to know how the Germans knew about the treasure. The Dutch people haven't found it but they know where it is. Tomorrow they have hired a huge crane and will attempt to raise a sunken boat from the river just outside.'

'That will be the German E boat opposite. The landlord was telling me earlier about the boat but he never mentioned any treasure. He also said there was a Dutch family staying here, mum, dad and two children as well as two German fishermen.' Kit related briefly his conversation with the landlord.

Pauline was giving a running commentary. 'One of the Germans has produced a gun and has threatened to harm the girl unless they get a share of the treasure. The children appear not to be there at the moment.'

'The woman's speaking again.' "Let's wait until we've found the treasure. We agree to split the proceeds. You can have two sixths and we will keep four sixths as it is really ours and there are four of us." 'They continue to argue but at last the Germans have given up and have gone back to their own rooms, slamming the door behind them.'

Kit spoke. 'Well one thing's pretty certain. The heavy crane will have a tough job getting into the field and down to the river because of all this rain and an even tougher time trying to lift a water-filled boat. Also I think we should call the police first thing tomorrow and put them in the picture. We can't have foreigners causing trouble in the peaceful British countryside.'

'Goodnight Kit. We really must try to get some sleep. It's only 3.0 o'clock.'

Eventually they did sleep but woke up about 6.30 when Kit made them a cup of tea with the proverbial Teasmade. 'Shall we have breakfast in the restaurant or shall I cook you egg and bacon on the launch?'

''We'll have it in the pub. I think we need to be ready to move when the crane arrives or when these characters show themselves. All is quiet at the moment. Maybe they've killed each other. I don't suppose we dreamed last night did we?'

'I certainly didn't dream that but I dreamt that I slept with a beautiful naked woman. I certainly enjoyed my sleep and feel fully recovered from my fall yesterday.'

'You get dressed in the bathroom while I get into my clothes in case you have any other desirable thoughts.'

Kit, with a broad grin on his face, got out of bed, grabbed his clothes and did his best to cover his nakedness. He washed and dressed quickly and returned to the bedroom. Pauline was just putting the finishing touches to her hair. Kit went over to her, kissed the back of her neck, then took one of her hands and knelt down on one knee and said, 'Pauline, I'm sure you know I love you. Will you please marry me.'

Pauline turned to look at him. 'Get up off the floor.' She also got to her feet, and pulling his face towards her and kissed him with a passion that gave him his answer. 'I'd be very honoured to be your wife. Are you sure that you're fully recovered from that bang on your head. What am I going to do with you?'

'I don't know but I think it'll be a job for life.' They held hands for a few moments and kissed once more. Then Kit brought them down to earth. 'Come on, we have work to do. I'm going to phone my friendly policeman, Chief Inspector Simpson and see if he can come over here in plain clothes. I'll also try and get Brian Chalmers. I'm sure he will know someone in the navy who might be interested in an ex-German naval vessel that someone is trying to salvage. I think our trip up the river will have to wait a little while. Do you mind?'

'Of course not. I shall always remember this weekend with you. All this excitement is too much for a poor country girl. Do you think there is any brandy on the launch? I may need some to steady my nerves.'

'I'm sure there is but you've had enough. I've suddenly had a bright idea. If all this can be sorted out by lunch time we could go to Canterbury to get your engagement ring. After all, they don't need us. We are innocent bystanders. Let's go down to breakfast.'

'What a lovely idea. You do have some nice thoughts, about the ring I mean.'

They had just ordered breakfast when the other guests began to arrive. Kit greeted them, 'I think it's going to be a fine day after all that rain. Wasn't it awful?'

The woman returned his greeting. 'Good morning. We're over here from Holland for a few days. It's a bit late in the year for a holiday but we're farmers and have to take time off whenever we can. This is my husband Hans and our two children Grechen and Gustave.'

Just then, two men walked into the restaurant. Kit said, 'Good morning,' and was greeted by two rather brusque replies as they nodded to the Dutch family.

With all the guests assembled Kit made his excuses and thought it a good time to phone the police and Brian. It took some time to get through to the chief. Everyone wanted to know what it was all about. In the end Kit said, 'I don't want to sound mysterious but if you'd just tell him it's Christopher Tynan and I have an urgent message for him I think he'll speak to me.' He heard a few clicks on the phone and then Simpson came on the line.

'Hello Kit. I dread to think what you've found this time. Spill the beans.'

Kit told him as briefly as he could and the fact that he had already told Brian Chalmers who might have a contact in the navy. 'I'm sorry to rush you but if you could be here by 10.30 we could have a quick coffee and then I have to go to Canterbury.'

'I'm on my way and will leave orders for the heavy gang to follow, incognito. We'll wait nearby for the heavy crane to arrive. That bit is interesting. We usually have movement-orders for large vehicles and so far nothing about a crane going to Plucks Gutter. Why are you there?'

'I'm on my holidays, just minding my own business – honestly. See you soon.'

'Goodbye.'

Chapter 23 — Salvage Operations

Kit returned to the dining room and said in a loud voice, 'Are you ready darling? We ought to make a move if we are going to Canterbury.'

'Just coming, dear.'

Kit spoke to the Dutch family. 'I suppose you'll be visiting Canterbury. It is a wonderful old city. I expect you know it goes back to Roman times. Very busy and the parking is difficult. We are hoping to avoid the traffic by going on the river.'

The woman, Kit now remembered her name, Gerda Angells, replied. 'We intend to go there later but this morning we are going to wander around locally.'

Kit and Pauline left the room and went upstairs to their bedroom. As they entered the telephone rang. It was the police. Kit immediately said, 'This line is not secure.'

Chief Inspector Simpson replied, 'That's OK. I thought you'd like to know we found a large crane coming your way. Apparently it has a very tricky job to do and because of all the rain has got a whole lot of steel strips to put over the ground. I thought you'd be interested. I'll be with you about half past ten.'

'That's fine. Thanks for letting me know. I look forward to seeing you. Cheerio.'

Kit had just replaced the receiver when it rang again. This time it was Brian.

'Hello Kit. I've followed up your suggestion about the navy so wheels are in motion. Not sure who we'll get but they are definitely interested, but it will probably not be today.'

Kit interrupted him to advise him that the line was not secure. Brian understood. 'OK. I'm getting used to cloak and dagger stuff when you're around. Expect me for coffee in about half an hour.'

Kit then went down to find the landlord. 'Sorry about the phone calls.' All part of the service Sir.'

'Some friends are coming over for coffee and maybe staying for lunch. I thought I should warn you. Can you give me the bill for our room and thanks for sorting out my clothes last night and helping my fiancée.' The landlord mentioned his other guests. 'The Dutch family are nice and friendly but the Germans are a bit sullen. It is strange. They are supposed to be here for the fishing but they don't seem to have any gear with them.'

'Maybe they thought you would hire out some. I suppose the real anglers always use their own and make their own bait.'

'Mine's not to reason why. I just provide bed and board and take their money.' he said with half a smile. 'Thank you Mr Tynan,' as Kit gave him a cheque.

Kit returned to the dining room, told Pauline he'd paid the bill and suggested that they should move their stuff back to the launch. They could come back to the coffee lounge when their friends arrived.

On their way Pauline explained that she had been in conversation with the Dutch woman who was very pleasant but did seem worried about something. Pauline had explained her interest in languages and they had conducted their conversation in Dutch.'

Simpson arrived with another man, Inspector Morrison. Kit ushered them into the coffee lounge and called Pauline to join them. The chief made the introductions and brought them up to date regarding the crane. 'Our traffic people came across it on the Thanet Way and waved them into a lay-by. It seems they were contacted by the Dutch Embassy in London and asked to go to Plucks Gutter to meet a Mr and Mrs Angells. They wanted a partially submerged boat lifted out of the river, transported to a nearby field, pumped out of water and eventually cut up for scrap. All the paperwork was in order so we couldn't really detain them but in view of your overheard conversation we've put one of our men on the transporter.'

'I'm going to have a word with the landlord and tell him we are checking up on aliens. So we may come and ask to see your passports or something that identifies you. We'll play it by ear from then on.'

A few moments later he returned with the landlord and the hotel register just as Gerda and her children came in. 'Mr Tynan. You booked in here last night. Do you have any means of identification?'

'Yes. My press card with a passable likeness.'

'Miss Matthews?'

'I don't have anything. Oh yes. My student's card. I'm at Canterbury University.'

'Thank you.'

He moved on to Gerda. 'Good morning Madame. Chief Inspector Simpson. What is your name?'

'Gerda Angells and these are my children Gretchen and Gustav. My husband is around somewhere. We have our passports. Grechen, nip upstairs to my room dear and bring down my handbag and tell your father to come down and bring his passport and you may as well get both of yours. Thank you.'

As soon as the passports had been produced Simpson said, 'Thank you. We're looking for a couple of people.' Turning to the landlord he asked, 'Where are these people?' indicating two names in the register.

'They arrived late yesterday afternoon. They're here for the fishing and have booked in for three, possibly four nights. They were here at breakfast but I haven't seen them since.'

'That's OK. Thank you. Good morning.'

Loud voices from outside caused everyone to wonder what was happening. Kit was first out of the door. In the field on the other side of the river a huge crane on a low-loader had arrived. Men were shouting above the noise of the engine as they tried to steer it off and position it on to steel strips on the soggy ground. Its caterpillar tracks helped but it was slow going as the steel mesh had to be taken up after the crane had passed and re-laid in front to commence the process all over again.

Kit whispered to Pauline, 'Let's slip away darling. They'll be here all day.' They quickly left and went to their launch, checked it over, cast off and with a wave to the Dutch family and to Simpson set off for Canterbury.

It took until mid-day before the crane was safely in position and tethered by four large stakes to prevent it toppling over. The crew chief turned to his mates and was heard calling out that it was almost time for lunch. He went to the pub and asked to see Mrs Angells to get her to sign an operations document. He explained that the operation would take longer than they had planned. 'That vessel is 120 feet long and probably full of water and mud and it weighs 120 tons. If we attempt a lift it might break but not where we want it. Alternatively it might topple our crane. If it's alright with you we will cut it up into three sections and, hopefully, that might do the trick. It's a good job the three engines are no longer on board. We'll get everything ready and probably start work after lunch. We will hold the boat steady and pump out as much water as possible before the tide comes in again. With a bit of luck we might find the hole in the hull and plug it so that we can get on with the lifting.'

'We shall then take it to a field down the road, prop it up securely so that you can go and look for whatever it is you hope to find and then we'll start cutting it up. That will take at least two weeks.'

The police became suspicious of the scale of this operation and wanted to know why Mrs Angells was so interested and apparently willing to pay for it. Chief Inspector Simpson called at the hotel and asked to speak to her. She was evasive at first but the policeman was adamant. 'I'm sorry but I am not satisfied with your answers. Unless you can give me a better answer you will have to accompany me to the police station at Ramsgate.'

Gerda decided to tell him the whole story. 'I own the boat. In fact I stole it from the Germans during the war and brought it over to England with my husband. Actually the Royal Navy brought us into Dover and I eventually worked for the Dutch Embassy. They can verify this if you wish. Perhaps I should also tell you that at the time I smuggled over a large quantity of diamonds to help pay for the war effort, several million guilders in fact. There was one packet that I never had time to collect and after all these years I just wondered if it was still there. As I brought the boat over in the first place I loaned it to the British navy and have a receipt for it. I have it upstairs in my suitcase. Shall I get it?'

'I think that would be a very good idea.'

She returned with a framed document stating exactly what she had told him. The chief said. 'This looks authentic but I shall have to get it verified. It's a very interesting story madam. You will stay in or around the hotel and I shall do some investigating of my own.' It was an order as well as a friendly statement. 'What was the name of the captain on the document? Ah, here it is Captain Reynolds Thank you.'

Chapter 24 — Proof of Ownership

'You have been honest with me,' Mrs Angells. 'I shall be equally frank with you. I understand you had an argument with some Germans last night. I'd like you to tell me what it was about.'

'Somehow they got to know about the diamonds and have been following us all the way from Holland, although we didn't know about them until last night. They don't know the whole story but they have threatened to harm my daughter if we don't share the diamonds with them. They produced a gun so we agreed. Fortunately my daughter is not aware of the threat.'

'Thank you. Are these two gentlemen in the hotel?'

'No. They are over there talking to the men on the crane.'

'We have their names from the hotel register. Don't do anything. We will go and have a word with them. John, can you go over and collect Colin from the low-loader and ask him to join us here. We must also invite the men to come here. It's a routine check on passports.'

Gerda felt she should say something, 'Thank you very much. I feel quite relieved. This whole story can be checked with my embassy in London but I haven't kept in touch with Captain Reynolds so I don't know where he is.'

'Don't worry. Leave everything to us. I'll get a sergeant and a policewoman to come over here tonight but even that may not be necessary if we can put these men behind bars for a couple of days. Thank you for your help.'

Sergeant John Selwyn went off to instruct his colleague while the chief went out to his car to get in touch with his headquarters to send over a police van and have a German speaking interpreter to be standing by.

John Selwyn was very polite but approached the men warily. 'Excuse me Sir,' he said, addressing the older man. 'I need to ask you and your friend a few questions. This is my police card. It won't take long if we could go back to the hotel. Would you also come along Sir,' speaking to Colin.

The four men made their way out of the field, over the bridge and into the pub, John leading the way with Colin at the rear.

By this time the chief had advised Gerda to return to her bedroom, then greeted his potential prisoners, 'Good morning gentlemen. I'm Chief Inspector Simpson from Ramsgate. I'd like to ask you a few questions regarding your stay here. Do you understand English?'

'I understand a little,' replied the older man but not Mr Holsteinmer. I will answer for him. How may we help?'

The chief was an old hand at an apparently honest approach by a prisoner and with his prior knowledge of their nocturnal activities, albeit given by a potential hostile witness, he had already decided they were guilty but he had to continue according to laid down procedures.

'May I see your passports which are usually retained by the landlord until you leave. I understand that you took them back as you need them for proof of identity when you go to Canterbury to get some money.'

They produced the passports and while the chief scrutinized them closely he asked John, 'See if you can get some coffee for our German friends while I check these against the register.' He moved over to the window to get a better view of the entries and their signatures in the passports.

The two entries in the hotel register appeared to have been written by the same hand. There were minor differences but one signature flowed quite smoothly whereas the other started off upright and then gradually sloped the same way as the first. The chief was not an expert but he reckoned that a graphologist would easily spot the difference.

He returned to the two men, now drinking their coffee and asked why only one person had signed the register. The older man realised he had slipped up and hastened to explain. 'Yes. Sorry about that. My friend has slightly sprained his hand so I signed for him. No problem, surely?'

The chief ignored the question. 'One other thing. Did you sleep well last night in spite of the storm?'

'Oh yes. Very nice hotel. Very comfortable.'

'You didn't, by any chance, have occasion to leave your room and visit another room?'

No. Slept like a log as you English say.'

'Now that is very strange because I have another version of the night's events and they do not tally with what you have just told me. Do you know a Mr and Mrs Angells? I believe they come from Holland.'

'No. Do you mean the lady and gentleman and their two children who are also staying here? We met them in the dining room but do not know them.'

'Think very carefully before you answer my next question. Did you enter their bedroom last night and threaten them with a gun?'

'That is absurd.'

'Mr Webber and Mr Holsteinmer, I'm arresting you both. You will accompany me to Ramsgate police station where you will be charged with a passport offence, threatening behaviour and carrying a gun. OK Sergeant, handcuff them. While we are waiting for transport I will look through your luggage to see if anything else comes to light. Where is the gun now? I know passport photographs are not always a true likeness but looking at you again I'm not convinced that these are your passports. Have you anything to add? I will write out a statement for each of you when we get to Ramsgate that you will sign with your correct signatures and for the moment that will be all. Drink up your coffee? You have virtually remained silent to these charges. Is there anything you wish to say.?

Both Germans nodded their heads. Mr Webber replied, 'We do not know what to say. We deny completely everything you have said about us. We would like to have some legal representation. I believe we are entitled to that.'

The chief was obviously enjoying himself. For some reason he had taken an instant dislike to the two men though, until proved guilty, he must remain neutral but he couldn't suppress his innermost feelings. He didn't take to them. Some people do have that effect. It was partly their arrogant approach to the whole matter. They had admitted nothing so he really had nothing to go on apart from the passport and these days that didn't seem to carry too much weight with the judge – that is if the case ever came to court.

Mrs Angells, on the other hand, he was inclined to believe. Her story was so unbelievable it just had to be true. He appreciated that he had yet to have confirmation from the Dutch embassy and they still had to trace Captain Reynolds if he was still alive. His people at Ramsgate were looking into this. Sergeant Rosemary Johnson, had only recently come to Ramsgate from Birmingham. She was one of the new university entrants and had already proved her worth. If the navy man was too frail to come to Ramsgate she would be the ideal person to send to him and to jog his memory gently.

Chapter 25

The Captain's Testimony

It was a good morning's work. Things were slotting into place quite nicely for once. It was Brian who had tracked down Captain Reynolds without too much difficulty and had telephoned the policeman. The captain was alive and well, having retired from the navy in 1955. He was still fairly active and was the Commandant of the Sea Cadets at Dover It was a purely administrative job but he loved every minute of it. He gave lectures on seamanship to the young lads and lasses that usually ended with him relating some of his exploits during the war. He occasionally went to sea with them and organised training weekends on real live warships in today's depleted navy.

The prisoners were soon tucked up in custody and in two days' time they were brought before the magistrate who seemed to be impressed with the police. The men were kept in custody while their embassy was informed and they were able to obtain a lawyer to answer their case. They were not allowed bail because of the problem with the gun even though it hadn't yet been found. The police had returned to their room at the pub and made a thorough search. Under a loose floorboard in one of their bedrooms they had found two full clips of bullets.

Pauline and Kit had returned late in the afternoon from their shopping expedition to Canterbury. Everyone else had gone so the following day, having spent the night on board their boat, they continued on their journey downstream. Pauline joked occasionally about the extra weight she had to carry and that for some reason her left hand felt very heavy. Kit had been able to show his press card and Pauline, her student's card so he was able to pay by cheque at the jewellers where they had bought her engagement ring.

A week later there was a general gathering of interested parties at Dover. Kit said a brief farewell to his fiancée and joined the party as a bystander and possible witness if the need arose.

Chief Inspector Simpson, Brian, Kit and Sergeant Sally Johnson who was driving set off for Dover. It was intended to be an informal party to get to the bottom of this strange affair so the chief had suggested that they meet Captain Reynolds in a local hotel. The ex-navy man had other ideas. He suggested that they meet at the headquarters of the local Sea Cadets and they could join him for lunch afterwards. At 11.00 o'clock they drew up outside the HQ and were met by a very smartly turned out guard of honour. The young girl cadet in charge stepped forward and said, 'Good morning. The Commandant will see you now. Please follow me.'

Slightly bemused, they did just that. They went up a short flight of stairs, the cadet knocked on a door and a voice from within the room said, 'Come,' and she opened the door and ushered the visitors inside.

Captain Reynolds (RN Retired) rose to greet them. 'Welcome to my humble abode. We don't get many VIPs so we thought we'd push the boat out.'

Simpson stepped forward. 'It was a very impressive turnout. If we'd known we could have turned up in uniform. Good morning Sir. I'm Chief Inspector Simpson.' He then proceeded to introduce the others of his party.

'Make yourselves comfortable. We can have coffee, rum or for you landlubbers, whisky, before we get down to business. Afterwards I'd be happy for you to join me for a spot of lunch.'

Simpson said, 'This is a curious affair, some of which I can't reveal at the moment as it may develop into a court case. Let me take you back 23 years. What do you remember of a Gerda Blom and a German soldier called Hans Engels?'

'I remember them very well. They eventually got married. Used to send me letters and Christmas cards but they stopped so I assumed they had died although they were quite young when I first met them. They borrowed a German E boat and intended to bring it to England. We intercepted them in the Channel and brought them to Dover.'

'What happened next?'

'She went to work at the Dutch Embassy in London. He became a prisoner of war. I understand they had previously met before the war. During the war they met again on her uncle's farm and later, after the war, they got married. They have two children. I have their photographs but they are at my home.'

'An interesting story. Is it written down somewhere?' Simpson thought it should be, knowing how meticulous the navy could be.

'I made my report at the time, of course, but I've no idea what became of it. Somewhere with naval records no doubt.'

'Was there anything else unusual about Gerda Blom or Gerda Angells as she is now?'

'Don't think so. They thought quite highly of her at the embassy. I met the chap from the embassy a Mr L...can't remember his name. I should think he'd be dead by now.'

'Might his name have been Lemmer?'

'That's it. Strange name. Foreign you know.'

'Anything else you can remember of Mrs Angells or of the boat they came in?'

'That was a marvellous craft. Three engines. Very fast. Practically no armour plating but plenty of offensive weaponry. They could do more than 40 knots. Of course they relied on speed to come over, do what damage they could and then scarper.'

Simpson was getting a little cross. He had given the navy officer plenty of opportunities to tell him what he really wanted to know. Sergeant Johnson, said, 'Excuse me Sir. Do you think I could ask Captain Reynolds a question?'

'Yes. Please carry om.'

Sergeant Johnson rose to her feet, automatically putting her higher than the captain so that he had to look up to her. 'Good morning. Sir, I'm Sgt Johnson. I have been in touch with Mr Blom in Amsterdam. He told me a very strange story. I'm just wondering if you can confirm it.'

To all present around the table Captain Reynolds appeared nonplussed and decidedly awkward, wondering what the policewoman was going to ask. She continued, 'He told me that he gave his daughter some diamonds to bring over in 1943 to help the war effort. I thought it was very strange but he was adamant. I wonder if you could confirm it or even deny it.'

The captain considered his reply for a long time. 'Ah. Yes. Now I do remember there were some diamonds. The man from the Dutch embassy took them away.'

'Thank you Sir. There is just one other thing that Mrs Angells asserts. She says that she has a promissory note from the Royal Navy that she owns the E boat, that she loaned it to the navy for the duration of the war and that it was some sort of prize money for capturing it in the first place. After the war, if it was still in one piece she could have it back.'

The captain looked really uncomfortable but decided to come clean. 'It's all coming back to me now. It was a long time ago. She reckoned that she had earned the E boat as a prize of war. The Dutch chap suggested that I gave her a receipt for it and I went along with the idea. As a matter of fact I got one of my chaps to prepare a rather elaborate receipt and signed it on behalf of the navy. She seemed happy with it.'

'Thank you Sir. That confirms what we already know. I expect you'd like to present at the end of the saga.'

'I've no idea where the E boat is now.'

'We do Sir, and Mrs Angells has come over from Holland to claim it.'

'She hasn't still got the receipt has she?'

'No Sir. We've got it. Would you like to see it?'

'Yes. I'm sorry about hesitating earlier. I wasn't sure how much you knew about the diamonds. I mean I know it was quite a tidy sum and I know they were not declared at customs.'

'That's not all. She wasn't able to retrieve all the diamonds out of the boat so she's over here to try and get them now but there are two snags. The first is the fact that the E boat is a wreck and full of mud at a place called Plucks Gutter. The second is that two Germans have apparently followed her over from Holland and according to her are demanding a share of the diamonds. I'll just go and get the receipt from the car.' She went outside with a half smile on her face.

After she had left the room the captain remarked, 'You've got a very able officer there. I really wouldn't like to be grilled by her for long. I'd confess to anything even if I was innocent.'

The chief was visibly impressed. 'No hard feelings?'

'Of course not,' replied the captain.'

The sergeant returned carrying the framed receipt all neatly wrapped in brown paper and with a flourish, mainly for effect, she tore off the wrapping and showed the elaborate receipt with the captain's signature in one corner.

The captain said, 'Well done, Sergeant,' and shook her hand. The chief brought the meeting to a close. 'Thank you for your time Captain Reynolds. I think we've got all we need in the way of confirmation.'

'You're welcome. Are you staying for lunch?'

'Regretfully no. We still have a lot to do and I have some villains who need my attention. Thank you again. If you'd like to see Mrs Angells, she is staying in the pub at Plucks Gutter for a few more days. This is the telephone number. It's up to you.'

'Thank you.'

They left quickly and went back to the car. The chief was in a happy mood. As soon as they had reached the top of the long hill coming out from Dover he instructed the Sergeant, 'As soon as you see a reasonable eating place pull in. Well done lady and gents. I think a good morning's work calls for a 'spot of lunch' as the captain would say. My treat, but you Sergeant may only have half a glass of wine.'

Brian said, 'It's a pity you have a customs officer on board. I think I might just ask Mrs Angells to declare her diamonds.'

'Over my dead body,' quipped Christopher, and they all joined in the laughter as the car slowed down and turned into the car park of the Red Lion.

Chapter 26 The River Relents

The two Germans, still protesting their innocence, arrived at Ramsgate police station where they demanded to see a German-speaking lawyer and a representative from their embassy. The police did not find the gun although in the luggage they found several rounds of ammunition, judged by the police to be sufficient evidence to sustain the arrest.

In the meantime, back in the field next to the partially submerged E boat, the salvage team were taking things slowly and carefully. Although the water and some of the mud had been pumped out of the boat, the tremendous weight and the suction from the river gave the impression that the river did not wish to relinquish its prize.

The team got a man, suitable attired, and tethered by a safety rope, to climb on to the boat in order to attach a cable under the stern in front of the propellers and another one just in front of the forward cabin. Two more were placed under the mid section. With cutting equipment they started on the demolition job and were surprised how easily they were able to cut through the hull. Making sure that each section was securely tethered was the longest part of this operation. With the tide going out more of the boat was revealed with each passing minute. At last the foreman gave the signal to the crane driver. Slowly, oh so, slowly the front section began to rise from its watery grave. The E boat was one of the later types with a metal hull. They decided to cut two holes in the hull so cutters were quickly started up and water and silt, collected over several years began to pour out.

The lifting crane started again, fearful in case one of the retaining cables broke. The sun came out and brought a measure of warmth to the damp surroundings. Another halt and two more holes were cut in the hull. These were larger than the first two and more water flowed out. Nobody on the low-loader or the crane knew why the lady wanted the old E boat. They merely had a job to do and got on with it. They looked forward to a pint at the end and payment. This was their first job of this kind that they had tackled and they would no doubt talk about it for several weeks to come.

The foreman decided they would make another effort. This time the boat moved easier but the crane driver was not impatient. When it was almost out of the water he ordered two teams to be ready to loop cables over the stern and middle part and attach the ends to the low-loader. In this way he figured that if at the last moment the boat broke free they would stop it falling back into the river.

He then called for the low-loader to be put into position to receive its cargo. The crane man lifted each section only sufficiently to reach the other vehicle and then lowered it gently while the team eased them into place with blocks and tackle to hold it steady while it was moved into position in a field down the road.

It took three trips and while all this was going on there was silence and then spontaneous cheering as the final section was moved. The men had worked from 8.30 in the morning and it was now 5.0 o'clock and they were ready to go home. The tide began to turn and in another half an hour there would be a clear stretch of river where the boat had been.

Although it was beginning to get dark Gerda and her family walked over the bridge and into Thanet to take a look at the boat. It really did look a sorry sight not only with the wooden supports and the two retaining cables fore and aft to keep it upright but also with four additional holes in the hull. The foreman was very pleased that the main part of the operation had been completed without mishap. He came to meet the family. 'There's your boat Mrs Angells. I'll leave the ladder here so that you can use it to get on deck. Make sure it is always secured at the rail. We'll be off now and when you have finished looking it over give the company a call and a different gang will come and cut it up.'

'Thank you very much. You have all worked so hard. This is for all the men. There is a hundred pounds. Is that enough as a token 'thank you'?

'Thank you very much. That's very generous Madame. They are thirsty devils, Thank you.'

'Here's another £25. Buy some crisps to go with beer.'

'Thank you again Madame,' and turning to the crew he called for 'Three cheers for Mrs Angells.'

Gerda decided to leave her inspection until the next day. She would put on some old clothes and bring a torch and a few tools. The family had just reached the pub when they met the landlord coming to meet them with a message that the police would like a word. Over the phone Sergeant Johnson explained, 'This is just a courtesy call. The two Germans are in custody for the moment awaiting trial so you can sleep easy tonight. We shall not be sending anyone over to look out for you tonight but if you need to get in touch with us you can ring this number. One more thing, Captain Reynolds has the pub number and I think he may well like to come over and see you. I thought you'd like to know.'

'That is most kind of you Sergeant. Will you please thank everybody. You have all been so kind.'

'We were glad to help Madame. Sleep well. Hope you find what you're looking for.'

Next morning Gerda suggested to Hans that he might like to take the children on the local bus to Fordwich to see the ancient village and the ducking chair where they once tried witches by ducking them in the river. This was a pretext so that she would be on her own when she tried to find the hiding place on the boat where she had put the bag of uncut diamonds all those years ago. She managed to borrow a few tools and a torch from the landlord who, fortunately, didn't ask too many questions. With high hopes she set off across the fields. She secured the ladder and climbed on board. Although parts of the boat had been altered much of it remained the same so she was able to get her bearings. Carefully and holding on to the handrail she went down a few steps into the forward cabin, the former cockpit with all the controls. As her eyes became accustomed to the restricted light she took a few more steps and reached the bottom. By the light of the torch she could make out the passage-way leading to the cabins.

Gerda closed her eyes and tried to recall exactly where she had hidden the diamonds. After such a long time she didn't expect to locate the hiding place at once and later felt quite pleased with herself as she logically ticked off all the likely places. She remembered it was behind a bulkhead, easy to find yet not too obvious. She also remembered a pipe of some sort running along the top and a stopcock. In the first cabin she entered there was the stopcock.

She trembled with excitement. It surely couldn't be this easy. And it wasn't. The small clip that she had originally opened with ease was now corroded. Balancing the torch she used the big screwdriver in an attempt to prise it open. When this failed she hit the screwdriver with the hammer and was glad when the metal collapsed. She needed metal cutters which she didn't have but by using the hammer and screwdriver she was able to enlarge the hole and look behind the bulkhead.

She heard something slither all the way down to the deck and thought it might be a rat. Her second thought which turned out to be correct was that it, dislodged with her destructive efforts, was the bag of diamonds. Had it really fallen all the way to the bottom or got stuck part way? She had no way of knowing. Not wishing to admit defeat and loathe to ask for outside assistance she figured that the whole bulkhead might have become weakened with age. She gave herself an hour to dismantle the bulkhead and hopefully find the bag.

She started at the top where she had already made a hole and gradually worked downwards. The noise was quite deafening, being so close and in a confined space but she hammered away and was pleased with the holes she had made. With a pair of pliers she was able to grip a piece of metal and gradually pull away a whole section of the bulkhead. Now she was able to insert the claw hammer behind the skin and virtually tear the aluminium away from its stronger framework. By shining the torch into the cavity she was able to see the bag. It looked to be in one piece although one corner had been broken. Gerda was getting tired but she decided to continue for another half an hour. Stretching down as far as she could she managed to reach the bag. If she pulled, all the diamonds might fall out. She took a deep breath, got a better grip on the bag. It was wet and slippery but she eased it carefully upwards until she was able to use her other hand and then she slipped, dislodged the torch and found herself in darkness.

She was cold and ached all over but she had the diamonds if only she could get them out. She withdrew her right hand and managed to find the torch and switch it on. She eased out the bag from its hiding place and stuffed it in her pocket. She took a couple of minutes to recover from her efforts, then gathered up her tools and made her way to the deck and to the warm sunshine. On deck everything looked the same. Nobody had come near the boat. If one or two diamonds had fallen through the hole in the bag she couldn't be bothered. She felt she had most of them and quickly returned to the pub.

She met the landlord who, seeing the muddy state of her clothes, asked if she was alright. 'Yes thanks. I fell over. I'll go upstairs and clean up.'

Upstairs she took off all her clothes and got into a hot bath and then put on fresh clothes and put her old ones in a laundry bag. The bag of diamonds she put in the sink and carefully teased out the diamonds, washed them several times in warm soapy water and put them on a towel to dry. Then she borrowed one of her husband's handkerchiefs and tied the four corners together with the diamonds inside. Next she washed and dried the tools and took them down to the landlord. It was almost too late for coffee but she decided there was just time before her family returned. She was still drinking it when they arrived back from their bus trip.

'Come upstairs. I've got something to show you.' She opened the handkerchief and told them the story of the diamonds and explained that they were uncut diamonds but still quite valuable. 'You may each choose one and keep it so you will never be poor. The remainder will go back to grandpa.'

For a moment there was silence. Hans was the first to recover and remarked, 'You're a dark horse – after all these years and I never guessed.'

'I couldn't tell you in 1943 and after we got back to Holland there really was no need. I do hope you understand. I never thought we'd find them.'

The children were a bit quiet and then Karl who had just had his eighteenth birthday, said, 'We need to know more. You must tell the whole story and when I leave college I shall write all about it. You'll be famous.'

Lydia, now 20, put her arms round her mother, thanked her and said she would have her diamond made into a pendant so that it would always remind her of her brave parents.

Chapter 27

Wedding Bells

Christopher Tynan needed time to think. For the moment all his articles had been completed. Just as well, he thought, as the last week or so had been fairly hectic. In fact he felt that he needed a short break. He phoned Pauline and she sensed he was at a loose end.

'Why don't you come down to The Haven this weekend and if you come by train I could give you a lift on my bike,' she joked.

'I think your bike has done its job. The first time I held on to you as your passenger I was hooked. Thanks for the invitation – I'll decline the bike ride but I would love to come and see you and your family.'

Pauline said she was sure it would be alright. 'I'll ask Lucy Brooks if she can do my stint at the station for the whole weekend.'

'Say hello to your parents for me and thank them. We haven't had an engagement party yet so I wondered if we could all go to that restaurant in town where we went on your mum's birthday.'

'That is a lovely idea. I'm sure mum and dad will be thrilled. Cheerio. Take care. Love you.'

'Goodnight, my love. Love you too,' replied Kit.

He ended the call and immediately rang Brian Chalmers. They chatted for some time about things that brought them up to date and ending with Kit's news of his engagement. 'Not sure when we will get married. Pauline has to finish her degree next June so we shall probably wait until after that. As soon as I know I'll get in touch because I'd like you to be my Best Man. Do you think you could keep a day free? Sorry I don't know when.'

'My dear Kit. No problem. I'd be honoured and congratulations to you both. Before you ring off I was just about to phone you and you'll never guess what it was about. Stella and I are also engaged. Will you be my Best Man? We've fixed the date- 24th January next year.'

'Well I never. Congratulations Brian. I shall be very pleased to do the honours. Are you sailing away on your yacht for your honeymoon?'

'Not on my yacht but we've already booked a cruise to the Maldives. We fly out on 26th January and return on 14th February.'

'With better timing we might have made it a double wedding,' he said, smiling.

'I don't think that would have gone down very well. You know how ladies enjoy all the attention on their very special day.'

'Oh wise one,' replied Kit. 'You are so right. I'm going to see Pauline at the weekend so I'd better find a book on wedding etiquette in Ramsgate. Very pleased to hear your news Brian. Congratulations once more to you both. Give Stella my best wishes.'

'Sure and vice versa to Pauline. You make a lovely couple.'

Kit arrived at The Haven on Friday afternoon. Bert and Beryl had decorated the place outside with balloons and streamers and a huge banner over the entrance, 'Congratulations Pauline and Christopher' in letters a foot high. He arrived before Pauline and they made a great fuss of him. 'I do apologise,' said Kit. 'I really should have asked your permission first but things just happened and it seemed to be the right time. Pauline reckons it was the bump on my head. Anyway, I'm glad you approve.

Pauline arrived just after five and they had one of their special high teas. Kit told them he had asked Brian to be his Best Man. Bert had already agreed to give his daughter away and Beryl was to be the Matron of Honour. Pauline said she'd like her best friend, Julia, at the University to be the Bridesmaid. They began making tentative suggestions about who should be invited to the wedding and suddenly realised it was all a bit premature.

Beryl said that she and Bert had been asked to go and see Mrs Rose, a near neighbour for a short while. 'You don't mind do you?'

Kit suggested that as they hadn't had an engagement party he'd like to take them their favourite restaurant tomorrow evening and they accepted.

When Kit and Pauline were on their own they looked each other in silence for a few minutes and then they both started to speak at the same time.

'You first,' suggested Kit. 'I think we'd better take notes as I'm sure there's a lot to talk about.'

'Well I'm not pushing for an early wedding and I'd like to get my degree first but of course I'll go along with anything that you would like.'

Then Kit began by saying, 'I agree that you should get your degree first. Will you look for a job locally or away or even abroad. Then there's the question of where we should live. My flat in London is just about big enough for two or we could look around where you work happens to be, rent for a while and then buy. I can fit in with your needs. I can write anywhere but I think we need to have a base – a place we can call our own.'

'You have been a busy boy, thinking all this out,' replied Pauline with a smile. 'Early next year people will come down to the University looking for likely candidates for inter-view. I don't think I want to teach at any of the language schools although it may come to that. I think I'm pretty good at languages. I speak French, German, Dutch and with Swedish I can just about get by in Danish and Finnish. If I get a grant and stayed on at university I'd like to learn the Baltic languages, Estonia, Latvian and so on.'

'There's a lot to think about', replied Kit. 'I shall be very proud to marry such a gifted young lady.'

'Not so young any more. How old do you think I am now?'

'That's not fair. If I say 20 I shall be accused of cradle snatching. If I say 40 I shall probably get my ears boxed. How much do you weigh? Kit got up and asked Pauline to stand beside him. He lifted her up. 'I reckon you weigh 9 stone 5 lbs – that should make you 25 and seven months.'

'Put me down,' said Pauline, laughing. 'How on earth did you know that. Mum must have told you. I'm actually 9 stone and 7 lbs and I really am 25 and a half. My birthday is in March so if we get married after that I shall be quite old.'

'That's alright because you will be marrying an old guy. I shall be 34, not quite old enough to be your father.'

'That's settled then. Degree first and I shall be a June bride and we'll worry about getting a job later and where we are going to live. In the meantime, being practical, can you afford to keep me in the style to which I have become accustomed. I could always get a full time job at the station,' said Pauline in a playful mood.

Kit was serious for a moment. 'These things do need to be discussed. I do have a steady job and a personal pension although it costs the earth but it's worth it. I also have a few thousand pounds in the bank and I have an endowment that should mature when I'm 40.'

He went on, 'What else do you need to know. I don't smoke. I drink a little but I don't like beer and I have all my own teeth.'

'So I'm marrying a perfect man,' laughed Pauline. 'What do you need to know about me?'

'Absolutely nothing. I love you just as you are.'

'Come here you lovely man. You do say the nicest things.'

Kit moved over and sat next to Pauline on the sofa. Just then they heard the key in the lock and a voice called out. 'It's only us.'

'Hang on a minute mum, we're just getting dressed.'

Beryl just managed to hear what she said and came rushing into the room. 'You wicked girl.' She addressed Kit. 'Do you really want to marry such a creature'

Kit got up. 'Yes please. I know I should have asked you and Bert first but it just happened and I don't regret it.'

'Come here son.' Beryl beckoned Kit to her. She kissed him. 'Bless you,' she said and ruffled his hair and then said, 'What have you done to your hair, Bert's just coming in.'

If Kit was a little embarrassed before he certainly felt a bit more uncomfortable now and turned to Pauline. 'Now see what trouble you've got me into.'

Pauline was quick to reply, 'Well at least you didn't get me into trouble.'

Beryl intervened. 'Stop it Pauline and go and make a pot of tea.'

Kit saw the funny side of the situation as he tried to smooth down his hair. In years to come he would remind Pauline of the incident. She said, 'I am really sorry Kit. I do apologise. I don't know what came over me.'

'Think nothing of it. I'll bide my time but I'll get my own back.'

When Bert came into the room he was all smiles. 'Your mother and I have been talking about your wedding. It's your big day Pauline. There will be no financial worries. Everything is on the house as it were. You may have the reception here or anywhere else. We are just about in the parish of St John in Margate, where you were baptised or there is always Canterbury cathedral for the wedding. For a wedding present to you both you may have the yacht and there will be a little bit of cash.'

'That's very generous Bert,' said Kit while Pauline jumped up and ran to her father and hugged him.

Beryl brought them all back to reality. 'Well that's settled. We have plenty of time to think about details like when, who is coming and the wedding dress. There really is a lot to do. We just wanted you to know we will take care of everything but I promise not to be intrusive.'

Bert, ever the practical one, said, 'Right let's have a nightcap and go to bed.'

Pauline looked at Kit, 'You've never seen my bedroom have you. If you're very good you may come and kiss me goodnight before you go back to your room.'

'Let's get married tomorrow,' replied Christopher.

In the space of six months there were two important weddings. No sooner had the Christmas festivities died down than Stella and Brian had their nuptials. It was huge affair with many of Brian's colleagues and friends present, either at the church or at the reception which was held at the Viking Hotel in Pegwell Bay. The police were well represented and there was a good contingent from the customs fraternity. Brian's mother came over from Whitstable and stayed overnight at the local hotel with Brian. Captain Reynolds and his wife were also invited. With many of Stella's friends as well as Kit and Pauline it seemed that the only people not there were the villains that had not yet been sent to prison and the people from Holland.

Not long after this event Pauline and Kit were married with many of the same people among the guests. Kit had many acquaintances but he only invited Max Sutherland from Capital News. Purely for sentimental reasons they decided to spend the first few days of their honeymoon at the hotel at Plucks Gutter. After the reception, held at The Haven, everybody went down to Ramsgate harbour and saw them off in the launch. It had been renamed Pauline and Bert had jokingly said. 'One Pauline is enough to handle. I don't know how you are going to cope with two. Best of luck, son!'

Author's Note

The characters in this book have been hidden by pseudonyms. Plucks Gutter is a little off my beaten track so I haven't been there recently but I believe the E boat is still stuck in the river mud. In fact it was never lifted out nor was it cut up. That part of my story is quite untrue. Gerda Angells was more than happy with the diamonds that she was able to retrieve and the elaborate receipt given by the navy for the E boat is on display in her study back home in Holland.

LM 2011

Len Manwaring

Len Manwaring served as a pilot and flying instructor during World War II and now lives in East Sussex.

He has also written the following books:

Alone: a wartime story of survival.

The Nelson Touch: a pilot's tale of WW II

Inheritance: a smuggling story of today.

Brylcreem and Black Ties: an autobiography

A Pebble and the story of a Cat: the story of a cat who talks

Lysander Landing: a novel of World War II